THE LIFE PATH

A CHRISTIAN'S GUIDE TO DISCOVERING GOD'S PURPOSE, CREATING YOUR LEGACY AND LIVING WITH PASSION

DR. THIEN DOAN

THE LIFE PATH

A CHRISTIAN'S GUIDE TO
DISCOVERING GOD'S PURPOSE,
CREATING YOUR LEGACY,
& LIVING WITH PASSION

DR. THIEN DOAN

The LIFE Path:
A Christian's Guide to Discovering God's Purpose, Creating Your Legacy, and Living with Passion

Copyright © 2017 by Thien H. Doan

All rights reserved. Printed in the United States of America. No part of this book may be used or reproduced in any manner whatsoever without written permission except in the case of brief quotations embodied in critical articles or reviews.

For information contact:
www.thiendoan.net

Book and Cover design by Thien Doan
ISBN-13: 978-1546621744
ISBN-10: 1546621741

First Edition: July 2017

10 9 8 7 6 5 4 3 2 1

CONTENTS

INTRODUCTION 3

CHAPTER 1 – The Problem of Wandering 17

CHAPTER 2 – The Prerequisites for Change 38

CHAPTER 3 – The 52-Day Miracle 53

CHAPTER 4 – The Path Principle 71

CHAPTER 5 – L is for Legacy 87

CHAPTER 6 – I is for Intentionality 114

CHAPTER 7 – F is for Focus 130

CHAPTER 8 – E is for Execution 151

CHAPTER 9 – Next Steps 177

WANT A FREE RESOURCES?

Go to my website:
thiendoan.net/resources

Visit my website for additional FREE resources:
- PDF download of "The LIFE Path Guide"
- Hours of videos of Thien's teaching
- Downloads of PowerPoint slides and notes
- Additional of Workshops & Seminars
- FREE books and resources
- And more to come...

INTRODUCTION

***

Ecclesiastes 12:12 says, "Of the making of many books there is no end." So why another book on productivity and life planning? If you are reading this book, you're probably stuck or wandering in some area of life. It's okay. I understand what that feels like. That's why I wrote this book. I'm writing this book for you and my friends who are also struggling to find traction and motivation in life. If you are looking for purpose and direction, I think this book can help you find your way.

The principles in this book have the power to change your life. And that's not an overstatement. I know this is true because these principles changed my life and the lives of hundreds of others.

There are plenty of books out there on this

subject by experts and success gurus who have conquered the world, made fortunes, and have millions of followers, fans and 'friends' on Social Media. I'm not one of them.

I know what you're thinking. You're wondering, "Who are you and why should I listen to you?"

That's a great question. My wife and kids ask me that all the time. Although I can't convince you that you should listen to me, I know I can help you. It's up to you whether you listen and apply my advice or not.

So, let me tell you a bit about myself. I believe I can help you because I've been where you are. I've spent many seasons stuck or wandering too.

I don't see myself as a success guru or anything like that. I'm skeptical of guys who promise that they can change your life. They can't. But you can change your own life.

I'm a fellow pilgrim on the road. I've had many challenges and ups and downs. For me, life wasn't (and isn't) easy. But I think I've done pretty well for myself. I'm content and filled with gratitude. I'm especially grateful for my many mentors that have helped me overcome challenges and obstacles along the way.

Indeed, there have been many challenges and

obstacles in my path. I am an immigrant from South Vietnam. My family came to America as refugees from the Vietnam War. My dad flew F-5s, my mom worked at IBM in Saigon, and my aunt and grandmother worked for U.S. Military Intelligence.

As the war ended, we were evacuated with the American military from Saigon. I had just celebrated my first birthday when we boarded a C-5 Galaxy transport plane for Guam, then eventually to a refugee camp on the Camp Pendleton Marine Corps Base in sunny southern California.

Being an immigrant has its own unique challenges. Add poverty, refugee status from an unpopular war and a dysfunctional and broken family and you get some difficult obstacles to overcome.

I'm also not the smartest or most talented person you'll meet. I struggled all through school. In fact, I nearly dropped out of High School. They stuck me in the remedial classes made up of gangstas and pregnant girls. Mrs. Wakefield was a portly, middle-aged version of Michelle Pfieffer from the movie *Dangerous Minds*, begging us to stay in school. I think Coolio was in the back of the class writing the lyrics to *Gangsta's Paradise*.

I missed over an entire grading period my Senior

year but still "graduated" with a cumulative grade point average of 1.6 (out of 4.0). The funny thing about my GPA is that because of the low graduation rate in South Los Angeles, I finished in the top half of my class! I guess I'm somewhat thankful that I went to one of the worst school districts in the nation. As Randy Newman sang, *I love L.A.*!

I worked throughout High School and college in restaurants, retail stores and doing clerical work through temp agencies. The greatest gift my immigrant parents gave to me was the value of hard work and tenacity. I knew that I wasn't going to get anything for free. If I wanted something I had to figure out a way to get it on my own. I'm a scrapper. I'm like Steve Rogers before he got the Super Soldier serum that turned him into Captain America. Beaten up and with a bloody nose, I'll still square up and look life's obstacles in the eye and say, "I can do this all day."

By the way, it might be helpful to mention that one of the reasons I struggled in school is that I have severe ADHD. I literally couldn't sit still. I talked constantly. I couldn't pay attention and I forgot my assignments. I was often sent to the Dean's office, put on detention and suspended from school because my teachers thought I was willfully opposing them or disrespectful of their authority. I was called lazy and dumb so much I guess I started to live it out. Also, it was during those years that I was dealing with the wounds of my family breaking apart and my mother leaving us. School just wasn't a priority.

Somewhere during those years, I found God. Actually, God found me and I "got saved" in a Baptist Church. That was a big deal to my Buddhist dad and he didn't talk to me for awhile. Of course, that wasn't that big of a change because he wasn't around much anyway.

During my four years at a two-year community college, I found a calling to serve God and others in ministry. I transferred to a Bible College and got a bachelors' degree (the first in my family). Then I went on to seminary and earned a master's degree. And I have just earned my doctorate. (I would have completed the doctorate much sooner but found my nemesis in Kate Turabian and her dreaded *Chicago Manual of Style for Research Papers, Theses, and Dissertations*.)

Today I'm a pastor, author, life coach, strategist, speaker, and many other things. I have been invited to speak to crowds all over the country and around the world as large as 6,000 people. My ministry travels have taken me to countries like France,

Australia, Israel, Cambodia and even back my native homeland of Vietnam to train church planters. I've started businesses and non-profit organizations.

The work that I have enjoyed the most is the starting of new churches. I have started and led three churches myself and helped to train, equip, and fund the start of dozens more.

Although my work has been fun and fulfilling, what I am most proud of is my family. I am married to my best friend. I am proud of the fact that I eat dinner with my wife and three children most nights of the week. I love being able to be home to cook dinner, help my kids with homework, and connect with my wife.

I am filled with gratitude that I'm living a life that I always wanted to live. Sure, life still has its challenges, but like Dave Ramsey likes to say, "I'm doing better than I deserve." Not bad for an immigrant kid from a broken home with ADHD growing up in the hood of L.A.

The thing that changed the trajectory of my life most was when I met my mentors. My mentors changed my life like Mr. Miyagi changed Daniel Larusso's. I found most of my mentors in the books I've read. The lessons these mentors have taught me have helped me overcome my personal obstacles and accomplish much more than I ever thought I could.

Although there have been amazing people who invested in me in real life, the greatest lessons came from words printed on a page. Stephen King says, "Books are uniquely portable magic." Through books, an author uses "telepathy" to transfer his thoughts, emotions, and insights across time and space to the reader. Books are a magical blend of time-travel, Vulcan mind-melding, and teleportation.

Through this *portable magic*, I have studied at the feet of the greatest minds and greatest people (note: they are not necessarily the same) in history. I'm a voracious reader. I love books. I read (or listen to) three to five or more books a week. The local library, Kindle Unlimited, Audible and the Overdrive App and I have become intimate friends.

I'm not an expert in psychology, human behavior, business, theology, ministry, or productivity. I'm not really an expert in anything. The only thing that I'm good at is reading and learning.

A long time ago, someone told me that "leaders are readers." I took that seriously and read the best books I could get my hands on. I am indebted to the many generous men and women who invested thousands of agonizing hours to use the *portable magic* of writing to transfer their wisdom and expertise into my life. These authors continue to influence and mentor me through their writing.

I don't have favorite authors or even favorite genres. I just read a lot. Along the way, I have picked up and treasured special morsels of wisdom from many different authors. None of the ideas that I present in this book are my own. I got them from someone else. But what is mine is how I organize and compile the many lessons into a portable and transferable package. They say that if you steal from one person it's called plagiarism. But if you steal from everyone it's called research.

I will attempt to distill and organize the many lessons that I have learned on personal growth and productivity into one helpful resource. I want to share with you what I've learned so you don't have to go through the time and effort of reading the hundreds of books on this subject as I did.

Each book I read gave a nugget or two of wisdom or practical advice on this subject. But very few are from a distinctly Christian perspective. Even though some of the authors are Christian, they don't overtly teach biblical principles because they are trying to appeal to the broader book-buying audience. I believe that there is an under-served niche of Christian people who need some practical advice on how to order and organize their lives.

Disclaimers

Before we dive in, I want to give you a disclaimer first. This book is written from a Christian perspective. Would you expect anything else from a pastor? Even so, I'm not assuming this will be read by Christians only. I've pulled insights from both Christian and secular authors and their books. I'm going to integrate the useful lessons that I've learned from both Christian and non-Christian sources.

Although I will lean heavily on the Bible, I believe readers from non-Christian or non-religious backgrounds will also find it helpful and encouraging. You don't have to be a church-goer or believe everything in the Bible to find these principles useful.

For you Christian readers, I want you to know ahead of time that I'm going to integrate lessons and principles from great thinkers in the fields of business, personal growth, management, psychology, sociology, and human potential. So, if you're one of those strict Christian readers that need to know the chapter and verse of the Bible each concept came from, you're going to be frustrated.

You may demand, "Where did you get this idea? Show me the chapter and verse of the Bible!"

I may answer, "Well, I didn't get this idea from the Bible. It came from Stephen Covey."

If you find that answer unacceptable, please do us both a favor and put this book down (and don't leave me a bad review on Amazon either). Just walk away. Maybe you can find something by Piper, Keller, or Spurgeon to make your soul sing instead.

Who Is This For?

So, who am I writing this book for? I'm writing this for my son Stephen who just turned 16. I love that boy! I see myself in him, poor guy. I want to help him navigate his life with an intentional path towards a great legacy. But like most teenagers, he doesn't think his dad's experiences are relevant to his life. When I try to share golden nuggets of wisdom during the short teachable moment during car rides or while helping him with homework he responds as I did at his age.

"Yeah, Dad. I know. Okay. I know that already."

I'm writing this for him, hoping that when he gets stuck in a rut or in a prolonged period of wandering, he will pick up this book and find some helpful advice and finally discover that his old man did know a thing or two about life.

[Stephen, if this is you finally reading this book, thank you. I want you to know that God has an amazing assignment for you! I love you son.]

I'm also writing this to help the members of my little church who are drifting through life. I love my church family. Currently, we have a lot of younger adults that are wandering through life without much intentionality. I want to help them discover and experience the abundant life Jesus came to give.

By extension, I'm writing this for you. I really want to help you. Thank you for giving me access to your life. I want to help you find your path to the life that you really want.

Promise and Preview

Here's my promise to you. I'm going to show you a system to help you stop drifting and find the path to the life you always wanted. The magic isn't found in personal strength or ability. The secret sauce is in the system. A good system will give you reliable and predictable results if you work it the way it's intended. All you need is a good playbook. In the following chapters, I will share my personal playbook on life that I have been using for over a dozen years. I call it *The LIFE Path*.

The famous coach of the Dallas Cowboys, Tom Landry, once said that the job of a coach is to "make someone do what they don't want to do so that they can become what they always wanted to become." In 2004, Brian Howard became my coach when I became a church planter and has become a good friend and colleague. One of the things that Brian made me do was create what he called a Life Plan that involved envisioning your desired future and setting goals. I thought Brian was a genius before I realized that he stole those ideas from Bob Logan and Michael Hyatt.

I've been using the Life Plan every year since then, editing and revising it each quarter. Along the way, I began to assimilate the new lessons that I've learned. In the following chapters, I will present to you what I call the *LIFE Path*. It's like the Life Plan, but mine is a pimped-out version with 22-inch spinning rims and bazooka woofers.

The word "*LIFE*" is an acronym for the four essential elements of personal growth and productivity:

L = Legacy
I = Intentionality
F = Focus
E = Execution

I devote a chapter to each of those concepts. I have used the *LIFE Path* in my professional coaching business and with the people in my church that I personally mentor. I teach it to leaders, pastors, and lay people. Each person has found these concepts to be useful and helpful. Some have experienced huge breakthroughs in personal growth and productivity through applying these principles. I think you will find it helpful as well.

Are you ready? Let's get started.

WANT A FREE RESOURCES?

Go to my website:
thiendoan.net/resources

CHAPTER 1

The Problem of Wandering

***

No One Gets Lost on Purpose

"Not all who wander are lost." I've seen that statement on t-shirts, posters and even on tattoos. It's sort of a conservative version of YOLO – "you only live once."

That statement was penned by J.R.R. Tolkien who was the author of *The Hobbit* and *The Lord of the Rings*. I'm not entirely sure what that statement even means, but he was probably referring to Hobbits, not the hipster struggling to find himself. HA! HA! HA!

Well, I guess Tolkien is technically correct. Not everyone who wanders is lost. Some wanderers are intentionally taking the scenic route in life. Not everyone who wanders is lost, but those that get lost usually get so by wandering. No one gets lost on purpose.

Some of Jesus' most famous parables are about things that get lost. A lost sheep. A lost coin. And a lost and prodigal son. None of these three became lost on purpose. The sheep probably got distracted from the herd. The coin was accidentally misplaced by its owner. The son chased the bright lights of the big city and found himself somewhere he didn't want to be. All three things got lost unintentionally and caused great pain and despair for those involved.

I've been lost or wandering in every way you can imagine. I've been lost geographically, relationally, spiritually, emotionally, and even vocationally. When you get lost, you lose your bearings and sense of direction. You stop and wonder to yourself "How did I end up here? This is not where I wanted to be."

Maybe you can relate. You've asked yourself, "Where am I? How did I end up here?" So many people are asking these questions today. How did I end up with these regrets? How did I end up with this relationship, or this career, or these hurtful memories?

So, if I wasn't clear earlier, let me restate the warning:

Wandering doesn't necessarily mean that you are lost. But getting lost usually starts with wandering.

What is Wandering?

For many years, my default setting in life was a frantic and exhausting mix of insecure drivenness, emotional reactivity, and a self-loathing withdrawal. I often bounced back and forth between being wandering aimlessly and being stuck in a ditch. Being stuck and wandering aimlessly are different experiences but they lead to the same result: zero progress.

When you're stuck, you are frozen by indecision or fear. You can't move. You're in a ditch on the side of the road with a flat tire. You feel helpless because you don't know what you should do. Should I change the tire? Do I have a spare? Do I know how to do it correctly? Should I call the Auto Club?

You're not sure what you should do, so you don't do anything. You just sit there. Waiting. You're not sure what you're waiting for, but you're waiting for something. That's what being stuck is like.

Wandering is a bit different. When you're

wandering, you are moving about from place to place. You're active, but you're aimless. You have no direction because you're not sure about your specific destination. You're not even sure you know your current location. But that doesn't stop your aimless wandering.

Sometimes the experience of wandering is a restful break from the drivenness of life. But we shouldn't make drifting a way of life.

You wander from relationship to relationship, job to job, even from church to church all the while lamenting with Bono, "I still haven't found what I'm looking for." That's a great song from my favorite album, but it's from the 80s and you should have found what you were looking for by now. The problem is you don't have a clue what you're looking for. And if you don't know what you're looking for, you're probably going to miss the path that will eventually lead to it.

It doesn't matter whether you're stuck in a ditch or drifting aimlessly, both will result in a lack of progress.

Wandering can be defined as moving about aimlessly or without direction. It is a rudderless boat drifting in the sea. We are currently facing an epidemic of wandering and drifting in our culture today. The currently reigning champions of wandering are the Millennials. To borrow a metaphor from Doug Wilson, if wandering were candied fruit, walnuts, and raisins, Millennials would be a three-pound fruitcake.

Abundant Life

One of my favorite verses in the Bible is John 10:10 where Jesus sums up why He came down from heaven to earth. This is His purpose. This is why He came. Jesus said:

> *The thief comes to steal, kill and destroy, but I have come to give you life and life abundantly.*

I love that word "abundance." The first picture that comes to my mind when I think of abundance is the Thanksgiving Table. Thanksgiving is my favorite holiday of the year because I'm a bit of a foodie. I love to cook, probably even more than I love to eat. Thanksgiving has all the family fun of Christmas without the added stress and expense of buying gifts for your kids.

Thanksgiving Dinner is a good metaphor for God's abundance because it overflows the bounds of just that one day. You have so much delicious food that you cannot possibly eat everything. Turkey, ham, and pot roast. Yukon gold potatoes mashed with butter, cream, and garlic. Stuffing made from home-made cornbread with breakfast sausage. Perfectly roasted Brussel sprouts with crispy burnt edges. Finished with strong coffee and a slice (okay, two slices) of Aunt Lynn's scratch-made cheesecake.

That's abundance. It's so abundant that you have to unbutton your jeans and loosen your belt because you ate too much. Then you fall helplessly into a tryptophan-induced nap with a blissful smile on your face.

Even though you ate as much as you could, you still have turkey and stuffing leftovers for days. And memories, love, and warmth that will hold you over until your family gathers again at Christmas. That's what God's abundance is like.

Jesus came to give us life. Not just any sort of life, but abundant life. He wasn't referring to subsistence-level survival or some spiritual state of consciousness in heaven after you die. He was referring to abundance in our lives here on earth. Abundant life doesn't refer to the quantity or duration of life, but rather the quality of life we experience.

Jesus was not promising a long life, but a life that will be filled passed the point of overflowing. It is a life that you are so thankful for because you have been blessed with so much more than you can contain.

I haven't met any Christians that would argue with me about whether God wants to bless His children with abundant life. Although there are probably some wackos out there picketing at a funeral of a fallen soldier who would disagree. But I don't think they read much and wouldn't buy this book anyway.

However, most Christians, including myself, would not describe our lives as being "abundant." Most of us are doing everything we can to survive, pay bills and raise a family. We are simply surviving, but not thriving.

Here's the big question we need to answer:

If Jesus came to give us abundant life, why are most of us not experiencing a thriving life of abundance?

Well, I'm glad you asked. Jesus tells us the reason right there in this verse. Right before He said that He comes to give us abundant life, He says that "the thief comes to steal, kill and destroy."

One paraphrase of the Bible reads this way:

The thief approaches with malicious intent, looking to steal, slaughter, and destroy.

Jesus was referring to His adversary, commonly known as the Devil. Christians believe that the Devil is a real spiritual being who was one of God's angels named Lucifer who rebelled against God. The Devil is described as a roaring lion who is actively seeking to devour followers of God. He is a thief and our enemy. However, since this is not a book on theology and spiritual warfare, we'll have to leave it at that.

Outwitting the Devil

Napoleon Hill wasn't a Christian, but he did believe in the Devil (sort of). Hill is the author of the bestselling success book of all time, *Think and Grow Rich*. Every success guru you ever heard of from Zig Ziglar to Brian Tracy to Wayne Dyer to Tony Robbins was influenced by Napoleon Hill.

In 1938, Hill wrote a book called, *Outwitting the Devil*. The book wasn't published until 2011 due to its controversial nature. His book is a fictional interview that he has with the Devil. It's an interesting read. It's sort of a personal growth, financial success version of C.S. Lewis' classic, *The Screwtape Letters*.

In this book, Hill interviews the Devil and forces

him to reveal his secret plans and tactics she uses to suppress and control people. While Hill is no theologian, he is extremely insightful about the nature of modern man.

The Devil confesses that his primary strategy to ruin the lives of people is to <u>"establish the habit of drifting"</u> in their lives. According to Hill, drifting or wandering aimlessly through life is the primary way "the Devil" seeks to control you.

This is Napoleon Hill's description of a drifter or aimless wanderer. Let's see how many of these statements could be said of you:

- You lack major purpose in your life.
- You conspicuously lack self-confidence.
- You seldom accomplish anything that requires thoughtfulness and hard work.
- You live paycheck to paycheck and your credit cards are maxed out.
- You complain when you suffer the least bit of physical or emotional discomfort.
- You have little or no imagination.
- You lack enthusiasm and initiative.
- You will not begin anything unless you are forced to.
- You take the path of least resistance whenever you can.

- You are often ill-tempered and lack control over your emotions.
- Your personality is unattractive to other people.
- You have opinions on everything but accurate knowledge of nothing.
- You are a "jack of all trades" but master of none.
- You repeat the same mistakes because you never learn from your failures.
- You are narrow-minded and intolerant, ready to argue with those who may disagree with you.
- You expect much from others but are unwilling to give much in return.
- You start many things but have completed few.
- You are loud in your condemnation of the system around you, but you cannot definitively say how it can be improved. (Translation: "You're a hater.")
- You are indecisive and avoid making decisions.
- When you are forced to decide, you will flip-flop at the first opportunity.

- You nit-pick and criticize others who are succeeding.
- You work hard to get yourself out of taking responsibility.
- You lie rather than admit your ignorance on a subject.
- You criticize others behind their backs and flatter them to their faces.
- You just accept what life throws at you without putting up a fight.
- You don't know what you want from life.
- You don't take responsibility for your life, but rather you prefer to blame others.
- You allow others to think for you because you are too lazy to use your own brain.

There are quite a few of those descriptions that apply to me. If I'm honest with myself, I must admit that I have spent a good portion of my life wandering and drifting aimlessly. How about you?

Three Types of Wanderers

There are so many people out there that are walking around with a low-grade fever of dissatisfaction and discontentment. They know that something is not right, but their discomfort is not alarming enough to get them to see a doctor. But not all wanderers or drifters are the same. I think there are at least three distinct types of wanderers. Let's talk about these three types of wanderers. See if one describes you.

Buffet Bob

Let's call the first type of drifter "Buffet Bob." At a time when so many opportunities abound, we are seeing less and less people pursuing life with passion and purpose. It's like going to an amazing buffet that offers everything you can imagine. There's everything from prime rib to seafood to lime jello.

Buffet Bob goes to this buffet and he walks around and around the buffet line. He wanders back and forth, looking at all the delicious food but never puts anything on his plate.

The myriad of choices causes decision paralysis, which is the fear of making the wrong choice. There's only so much Bob can eat and everything looks so good. Bob doesn't know where to start. If he chooses the prime rib, he won't have room for the salmon or the potatoes. Bob is stuck. He can't decide. Even when he does decide, he can't fully enjoy what's on his plate because he is second-guessing his choice because he has FOMO – the fear of missing out.

Perhaps the reason that Bob isn't putting

anything on his plate is even more nefarious. Bob is simply not hungry. He has been munching on Cheetos, instant ramen, and two-for-a-dollar tacos all day and has lost his appetite.

Buffet Bob is a description of the current mindset of many of my friends and relatives. They can't choose a career or a person to date or a church to go to, or whatever. They wander back and forth discontent. Or they have been doing the equivalent to eating relational junk food all day. When Mr. or Ms. Right comes along, they aren't interested. I honestly want to yell at them to "JUST PICK SOMETHING ALREADY!"

Are you a Buffet Bob? Lots of choices, but you can't decide?

Bubble Betty

If you can't relate to Buffet Bob, maybe you're a "Bubble Betty." When was the last time you played with bubbles? Imagine a three-year-old little girl playing with soap bubbles in the front yard. Can you see her in your mind's eye? Of course you can. We've all been this kid. Well, I had to make my own bubble solution with Dawn soap and use a chopstick and string for the wand. (Hey, don't judge me because I grew up poor!)

Imagine what is going on in Bubble Betty's mind when she is playing with bubbles. She is in her front yard with her momma on a bright summer day. Momma takes out the bubble wand and gently blows into it. Then magic occurs. The sky is filled with dozens of perfectly round balls of light floating all around little Betty. When the bubbles catch the sunlight at just the right angle, it refracts into a rainbow of glistening colors. That's pure magic to little Betty. She is transfixed and hypnotized by this new discovery.

What does Betty do next? Well, she decides that she's "gotta catch 'em all" like a middle schooler playing Pokemon Go. Bubble Betty runs around giggly with glee trying to catch a bubble with her hands. She thinks that if only she could catch one of these magical bubbles, then her life would be fulfilled.

Most of the bubbles are carried off by the wind beyond the reach of her adorably chubby arms. They seem unattainable to her. Luckily, the wind carries a bubble right in front of her. Betty reaches out to catch it and when she thinks she has it, what happens? It pops.

Undeterred, Betty chases another one and catches it. It pops. She catches another one. That one pops too. The cycle repeats. Chase. Catch. Pop. Rinse and repeat. This goes on and on until Betty is so tired she has to take a nap. Good job, momma. You're an evil genius for getting those soap bubbles to entertain your daughter while you sit on the porch with your iced tea.

Millennials are a generation of Bubble Bettys. They are fixed on the magic of the American Dream or internet millions or relationship bliss. They run from one bubble to another hoping to capture its magic because they believe that the magic will change their lives and bring fulfillment. They move from job to job, relationship to relationship, even church to church because they believe that the next one will contain that life-fulfilling magic.

Are you a Bubble Betty? Can you relate to the constant pursuit of something just outside your grasp?

Entitled Ethan

Probably the worst type of wanderer is "Entitled Ethan." One of the unlikely sources of drifting and aimless wandering is entitlement. Entitlement is the feeling that you are owed special treatment even though you did nothing to earn it. You see examples of entitled people on YouTube ranting, "I pay my taxes! I deserve to be treated better!"

The worst case of entitlement I've ever heard of comes from the Nation of Texas. In 2013, 16-year old Ethan Couch was at a party drinking and smoking weed with his friends. When the booze ran out, he decided to go and steal some more from the local WalMart. Ethan and his buddies jumped into his red Ford F-350 pick-up. It would be helpful to the non-Texans to know that the F-350 is the ultimate Redneck status symbol, equivalent to driving a Lexus or a Tesla in Southern California where I live.

With seven people inside the cab and two in the bed of the truck, and under the influence of alcohol and weed, Ethan recklessly races down the rural road at dangerous speed. Maybe he wanted to impress the girls in the car.

Up ahead, a family of three was experiencing engine trouble pulled their car over onto the side of the road. A local pastor saw the people in need and stopped to help. This is when Ethan's gigantic F-350 comes racing around the bend and smashes into the two parked cars and flips over and crashes into a tree.

Tragically, Ethan's actions lead to the death of the four people on the side of the road including the local pastor who stopped to help his neighbors. No one in the truck was killed, but one was permanently paralyzed.

But this is not the most tragic part of this story. Because Ethan was only 16-years old, the maximum sentence for four counts of "vehicular manslaughter while driving under the influence" would have been only seven years in prison. Since his family was wealthy, they hired expert defense lawyers to argue his case.

Ethan's attorney gave the most ridiculous defense argument in human history. He argued that Ethan should not be held responsible for the deaths, injury, and property damage he caused because he suffered from a serious case of "affluenza." If you've never heard of "affluenza" before, it's not your fault. It's a made-up word that combines influenza and affluence.

His lawyers argued that since Ethan was raised in a wealthy home that taught him to feel entitled to special treatment his whole life, that he did not have the ability to discern the repercussions of his actions. In layman's terms, they argued that Ethan shouldn't be punished because he is a rich spoiled brat.

Inconceivably, the court agreed with the defense and dismissed jail time and only gave Ethan probation for killing those four people while under the influence of alcohol and marijuana. I was in total disbelief when I heard of this news story. I thought it was from some alternate reality like in *The Hunger Games*. Texas, how could you?

In a semi-satisfying turn of dysfunctional events, Ethan's mom liquidized their assets and relocated them to the beautiful resort town of Puerto Vallarta, Mexico. Being the absolute reprobate idiot that he is, Ethan couldn't help taking selfies while playing beer pong in Puerto Vallarta and sending it out on Social Media. #idiot

Of course, the Mexican government didn't want this bad hombre in their country so they allowed the U.S. Marshals to come and collect Ethan and his mom. He was sentenced to two years in prison for parole violation. Not enough, but better than nothing.

Okay, you're not as bad as Ethan Couch, but you have to admit that you also struggle with a sense of entitlement in some area of your life. We all do. It's inescapable.

I feel entitled to respect from my kids, courtesy from the waiter, lack of e-Coli from Denny's. Is that too much to ask? You may feel entitled to not be harassed by the police, or for the teachers to actually help your kids learn. We all feel entitled to what Jefferson called "certain unalienable rights." But when these rights are not afforded to us, then there's a problem.

Entitlement leads to expectations. Expectations represent the minimum level that you are willing to accept. When our expectations are high, it leads to dissatisfaction. And dissatisfaction leads to wandering.

You may feel dissatisfied with life, but you don't know why. If you trace your dissatisfaction back to its source, you may find that it came from your high (maybe unrealistic) expectations which you have because of your sense of personal entitlement. Entitlement is destructive if left unchecked. It is cancer that can metastasize and spread throughout your soul.

Two areas that entitlement destroys most are gratitude and responsibility. If you believe that you are owed something just because you are you, you will never be thankful for what you have. Your sense of entitlement also excuses you from taking any sort of responsibility to achieve for yourself what you believe you already deserve.

Entitlement has a way of destroying relationships and even one's faith. This is an especially dangerous trap for Christians. American Christians are perhaps the most entitled people on earth. We believe that God owes us life, liberty, comfort, protection, prosperity, health, and the list goes on and on. This doesn't apply just to those who follow the "health, wealth and prosperity" teachers but to every American Christian I've met.

Have ever prayed, "God, how could you allow this to happen to me?" If you have, guess what? You have an entitlement problem.

When you don't get what you believe you are entitled to, you blame and question God. Your faith and confidence are rocked because God didn't give you something that you believed He owed you.

It is this sense of entitlement that causes many to wander through life. We feel entitled to certain things in a relationship and because your current love interest doesn't measure up, you throw him or her back into the pond and keep fishing. Your career is not satisfying your expectations, so you change your job or career field. Your church service doesn't make your soul sing every time you sporadically attend once or twice a month, so you look for another church.

Why all this wandering and drifting? Perhaps you have more in common with Entitled Ethan than you want to admit.

Summary

I hope you are coming to the realization that the whole matter of wandering and drifting is an internal problem, not an external one. To put it bluntly, *it's a YOU problem.* Your wandering is a symptom of a deeper soul problem. It's not a problem with your boss, or the government, or "the man." It's an internal problem that you will take with you wherever you wander off to next. Only once you realize this can you begin to make progress.

To fix any problem, you first must identify the problem. To stop drifting and wandering aimlessly, we must first acknowledge we are drifting and wandering. Only then can we begin to address this problem.

Wherever you go, there you are.

CHAPTER 2

The Prerequisites to Change

* * *

The Life Change Formula

When I was a student in Bible College, I considered becoming a foreign missionary to an unreached people group. I was inspired by the story of Jim Elliot and the five missionary martyrs in Ecuador. I heard Jim's widow, author Elisabeth Elliot, speak at a Missions Conference. She shared about how she continued the work her husband and his team had started and eventually reached the entire village for Christ. Even the men who killed her husband became followers of Jesus.

This conference was supposed to be a recruitment event for Christian Missionary agencies to get young impressionable and naive Bible College students to spend their summer break building homes, digging wells, or leading kids' programs on the mission field around the globe.

I was so ready to sign up. I wanted to go to a difficult place like Jim Elliot did. I had this romanticized picture of life on the mission field from the books that I read. I guess this is a little like what fans of Louis L'Amour feel about the Old West, as they pine with nostalgia for a place they had never been before.

But then Elisabeth Elliot destroyed all that for me. What she said gave me pause and forced me to reconsider becoming a missionary. This is what I remember her saying:

> *Most of you shouldn't become missionaries. It's really hard. Most of you wouldn't make it. You would quit and go home in a month. You should not even consider becoming a missionary unless you have already endured significant pain and hardship in your lives. Pain is a prerequisite for the mission field.*

According to Elliot, the ability to endure pain is a

prerequisite for the mission field. She had seen too many enthusiastic and well-intentioned young people quit after a few weeks because they couldn't endure the hardship of the assignment.

In a similar, but not as extreme, way of thinking, I want to warn you about the prerequisites for our journey together on the *LIFE Path*. I don't want to sound harsh or be exclusive, but I do want to inform you about what is ahead.

We're going to take a journey together. I believe this journey will improve the quality, and maybe even change the trajectory, of your life. But not everyone who begins this journey will complete it. I just want you to know what you're getting into before we get started.

There are three prerequisites for this journey. These are things that you need to have before you can begin. If you don't have these things, it's better not to even begin because you will not finish. Before we start this journey together, we need to do a gear check. You wouldn't want to go mountain climbing without first checking to see if you have the right equipment, would you?

There are three things that we need to check before we begin. These three prerequisites make up something I call *The Life-Change Formula*.

The three prerequisites are dissatisfaction, vision, and responsibility. Just think of a DVR.

Dissatisfaction

The first prerequisite is *dissatisfaction*. This is the starting point. Change begins with dissatisfaction. You cannot change anything that you are willing to tolerate.

In John 5, we see a story about Jesus visiting the Pool of Bethesda. This was a sad sight. This beautiful pool became the daily meeting place for dozens, maybe even hundreds, of sick, diseased, and crippled people. The sick were outcasts in that society and forced into a life of begging. That culture believed that sickness was a sign you did something wrong and God cursed you because of it. And to help a person cursed by God would be to incur that curse upon yourself.

I imagine the scene of the Pool of Bethesda to be like San Pedro and San Julian streets in downtown L.A. Those streets are called Skid Row and is where the largest community of homeless outcasts in the nation find community and a little bit of hope.

The poor souls waiting around the Pool of Bethesda were there because of a superstition. They heard the rumor that a sick person could be healed by the waters of the pool when an angel stirred the waters.

Jesus approached a man who has been crippled for thirty-eight long years. Jesus asked him a simple and obvious question, "Do you want to get well?"

Excuse me, Mr. Jesus. Really? What kind of question was that? Jesus, you don't know? Of course, he wants to get well. He's been sick for thirty-eight years. Why do you think he's at the healing pool?

We would expect the crippled man answer Jesus' simple and direct question this way:

Do I want to get well? Hmmm. Let me think... Of course, I want to get well! I've been crippled for 38 years! I am so tired of this life! I want to be healed more than I ever wanted anything! Jesus, please heal me!

But that's not how he responds to Jesus' question. He responds by making excuses of why he is in the predicament he is in. He blames the other sick people who selfishly cut in front of the line when the water is stirred. "It's their fault!" he complains.

Of course, Jesus is much smarter that I am. He knew something about the hearts of men. He knew that it is impossible to live with a problem for this long a time and not get used to it. After a while, you accept it and begin to adjust, make excuses and compensate for your problems. This man had learned to get by and tolerate his problem.

We know that Jesus eventually heals this man and tells him to pick up his mat and walk home. But why did Jesus ask the crippled man such an obvious question before He healed him? I think the reason Jesus asked this question was to cause this crippled man to become dissatisfied with his current condition. He wanted him to imagine what wholeness and healing would be like.

Jesus asked him, "Do you want to be made well again? Do you want to be healed? How awesome would that be? Do you want that?"

Dissatisfaction is a prerequisite for life change. You cannot change what you're willing to endure or tolerate. You cannot change a troubled relationship if you are willing to endure it. You cannot change your negative habits if you continue to tolerate your own behavior. Change requires the catalyst of dissatisfaction.

Dissatisfaction is a seed of hope. We only become dissatisfied if we have hope that there is something better out there. Hopeless people are satisfied people because they do not believe change is possible.

This reminds me of a story I heard. Two country

boys sat on their front porch on rocking chairs enjoying sweet tea in the cool of the afternoon. A lazy old hound dog lay at their feet. Every so often the lazy dog would wake up and howl in pain. The dog repeated this strange behavior every few minutes.

"Why does your dog howl like that? Is he hurt?"

"Nope. He's jest layin' on a nail."

"Well, why don't he git up 'n move to 'nother place?"

"I reckin' it don't hurt him 'nuff yet."

Is this you? Are you like that hound dog? You don't like where you are in life. It's not comfortable. You complain about the pain and frustration you're experiencing because you have a "thorn in the flesh." But for some reason, you aren't ready to get up off that nail and find a better place. Hopefully, until now. Now is the time to make the change. Take the King of Pop's advice and look at the man in the mirror and ask him to make a change (A-Hee-Hee, Chommon).

There's a lovely lady at my church named Dorothy. She is a prayer warrior and sober addict that is involved in recovery ministry. When addicts come to her wanting to change, she would say, "You can't change until you become sick and tired of being sick and tired."

Dissatisfaction is the beginning of change. It's a prerequisite.

Vision = Clear & compelling picture of a preferred future

The second prerequisite for our journey is *Vision*. This builds on top of the first prerequisite of dissatisfaction. Once you become dissatisfied with where you are, you need to have a vision of where you want to go.

A simple definition of vision is a clear and compelling picture of a preferred future. It's a picture of the life that you want. For this vision to be effective, it needs to be both compelling and clear. An unclear vision is not compelling. Vague desires for a better life won't get your butt off the couch.

Vision must also be compelling. It must move you emotionally. The image of your preferred future must be so attractive that it draws you in like a bee to a yellow flower. It needs to be something that captures your heart and imagination, something that you long and thirst for. This vision of a preferred future has to be strong enough to break the gravitational pull of the couch and entice you to get off your butt in pursuit of this dream.

It is difficult to thrive when you don't have a purpose to live for. Your purpose must be in

THE LIFE PATH

something bigger than you. <u>It cannot be something so small and inconsequential as your happiness</u>. If your goal in life is "to be happy," you can be assured that you will live a very sad and unfulfilling life. Because the things that make you happy are not the things that will bring you true joy.

What makes me happy is sitting in front of the TV and binge-watching Netflix and eating chocolate ice cream with BBQ potato chips (and yes, those do make a good pairing). But does that bring me true joy? Of course not. What follows is not joy but guilt and self-loathing and acid reflux.

<u>The things that bring true joy are not usually the things that make me happy in the immediate moment.</u> Working out, eating right, investing in relationships, being a good listener, volunteering my time at church, serving the poor, being generous and kind to those in need, etc. Those activities don't make me happy in the moment, but they bring the result of deep and lasting joy.

Pursuing happiness is a dead end. Instead, we need to pursue a life of purpose. Because without purpose, we become shallow Hedonists driven by the motto: "Eat, drink and be merry, for tomorrow we die."

Vision starts by understanding that God has a purpose and an assignment for your life. Ephesians 2:8-9 is one of the most beautiful explanations of how God saves unworthy people. God saves us "by grace through faith." Those two verses tell us how we are saved, but verse 10 tells us why we are saved.

For we are God's workmanship, created in Christ Jesus for good works which He has prepared in advance for us that we should walk in them.

Now that's a clear and compelling vision for your life. According to that verse, you are a masterpiece of God's creation. And God intentionally created you with a purpose in mind. He has a specific assignment prepared for you that He wants you to complete. He has marked out a specific path that you "should walk in."

That's a vision that will motivate you to turn off Netflix and get off the couch. You are a masterpiece of God! He created you with a purpose in mind. The Creator and Ruler of the Universe has a specific assignment for you!

Just think about that for a minute. Let your soul absorb this idea. Just think, what would it be like to live with that level of purpose? Can you imagine the confidence you would have? How would being used by God, to accomplish an assignment He crafted specifically for you, feel?

God has a clear and compelling assignment for your life. Can you see it? Is your vision clear? Is it compelling enough to get your butt off the couch?

[Margin note: *love how blunt he is!*]

Responsibility

The third prerequisite is *Responsibility*. Spider-Man's uncle taught him the life-changing lesson that "with great power comes great responsibility." I don't want to contradict Uncle Ben, but I think the opposite of that statement is also true and far more relevant to those of us that haven't been bitten by radioactive spiders.

> *With great responsibility comes great power.*

[Margin annotation: *without responsibility there is / you have no power/strength*]

There. I like that statement much better. Talk about a rare superpower. When was the last time you saw someone take full responsibility for their actions and choices, along with the consequences? We live in a spin-doctoring culture of "alternative facts" and blame-shifting.

Taking 100% responsibility for your life is a prerequisite for this journey. You can't blame someone else for your problems. You can't make excuses. You need to take full responsibility for your life.

Taking responsibility is rare today because it is so easy to blame others and make excuses. Everyone does it. So why can't I?

Jack Canfield, the *Chicken Soup for the Soul* guy, writes:

Most of us have been conditioned to blame something outside of ourselves for the parts of our life we don't like. We blame our parents, our bosses, our friends, our co-workers, our clients, our spouse, the weather, the economy, our astrological chart, our lack of money - anyone or anything we can pin the blame on. We never want to look at where the real problem is - ourselves.

Ouch! Dang, Mr. Canfield, did you have to be so harsh? I thought you only wrote encouraging stuff. That chicken soup was a little too hot. I think I burned my tongue.

Taking responsibility helps you overcome one of the biggest barriers in your path. That's the barrier of your excuses. Making excuses robs you of your power and makes you a victim and a passive observer of your own life. This is probably the biggest roadblock that hinders you from experiencing the life that God has in store for you.

Making excuses and blaming others leads to a perception of victimhood. You become a weak victim who is convinced that your problems and defects are caused by others. This frees you from any responsibility to do anything for yourself. When you make excuses, or envy and blame others, it leads you down the path to becoming a victim. You will begin to see yourself as a weak and helpless victim. You will say, "It's not my fault." Well, that may be true. Maybe it's not your fault, but it is your responsibility.

There's a big difference between fault, blame, and responsibility. Understanding the differences will help you embrace this idea.

To be responsible is to be accountable for a choice or action. To be at fault is to be the cause of a failure or wrongful act. To blame is to hold someone else responsible for that wrongful act. Sometimes we say, "It's not my fault" or we cast blame and say, "It's their fault!"

It could be 100% someone else's fault that you are in your current bad situation. Perhaps someone hurt you and you truly were a victim of their malice. It truly could be someone else's fault. You have every right to blame them.

But no matter whose fault it is, you are ALWAYS RESPONSIBLE for your own actions. If someone knocked you down and hurt you, it would be their fault. You could blame them as much as you want. But they are not responsible for picking you up.

Who is responsible for getting you back on your feet? You are. No one else. It may have been their fault you got knocked down, but it is your responsibility to get back up again. You need to separate fault and responsibility. They are not the same.

Author Mark Manson says,

Fault vs Responsibility

We are responsible for everything in our lives. We always control how we interpret what happens to us, as well as how we respond. Fault is past tense. Responsibility is present tense. Fault results from choices that have already been made. Responsibility results from the choices you're currently making.

Fault finding and casting blame are not helpful practices. They don't help you accomplish anything or make progress today. Finding fault is looking back to see who knocked you down. But that doesn't help you get back on your feet today.

The guy who knocked you down isn't going to

come back and pick you up. It was his fault you're on the ground, but it is not his responsibility to pick you up. <u>It is 100% your responsibility</u> whether you get <u>back up or wallow on the ground like a helpless</u> victim.

Summary

Before you can experience any real change in your life, set your <u>DVR</u> – <u>dissatisfaction</u>, <u>vision</u>, and <u>responsibility</u>. These are the three prerequisites for our journey together. You're not going to get very far if you don't set the DVR.

This is what people so often want – for the person who hurt them to come back and help them. Nope – it won't happen

2 choices
① Get Up or
② Wallow

CHAPTER 3

The 52-Day Miracle

***

Waiting for a Miracle

Have you been waiting for a miracle? How long do miracles take? How long are you supposed to wait before you give up and go home?

A paralyzed man waited for thirty-eight long years by the Pool of Bethesda for healing before Jesus came around. I spent twenty-seven years in prayer for my mother's salvation before she gave her life to Jesus three months before she died.

<u>I'm not sure how long you're supposed to wait.</u> But I do know that God can change your situation

quickly. Sometimes change takes place in an instant. Jesus shows up. The floodgates of heaven open up. Then BAM! Hallelujah! Thank Ya Jesus! IT'S A MIRACLE!

But other times (most of the time) God doesn't choose to accomplish His plan by means of unexplainable and instantaneous acts of power. More often, God works through committed people and intentional processes.

If God chooses to use an intentional process instead of an instantaneous act of divine power, can we still call that a miracle? Why not? I think so. I think we need to change how we think of miracles.

I would like to expand the ordinary understanding of the miraculous. This is how I have come to define miracles. I believe that a miracle is when God does the humanly impossible by means of His power, His people, or His processes. If we would expand our definition of what a miracle is to include God's use of His people and His processes, then we would see a world full of everyday miracles.

One of the primary purposes for miracles in the Bible was to validate the message of God to the hard hearts of doubting men. Moses and the Ten Plagues. Elijah and the fire from heaven. Jesus healing the sick. These miracles act as proof of the presence of

We really ALL want instant miracles instead of His intentional process

the divine. When we experience a miracle, we respond like Thomas, after he saw the Resurrected Jesus and touched His crucifixion wounds, saying, "My Lord and my God!"

I'm praying for miracles in my life. I need God to do the impossible in my life and in my family. I want to see God do the impossible in my church and my community.

I'm sure you have the same desire. You want God to breathe life into your soul. You want God to resurrect the dead faith in your life or in the life of someone you love. You want God to heal a terminally ill marriage. You want God to heal your blindness because you can't see where you're going in life. You want God to multiply your fish and loaves because you have so many mouths to feed.

So, you're looking for a miracle. You need God to intervene and do the impossible. I truly believe that you and I can see God do miracles in our lives today.

God promises to be with us and never leave or forsake us. Jesus says that He came to give us a life full of abundance. The Bible says that in the last days God is going to pour out His Holy Spirit on all people and we're going to see visions, dream dreams, and prophesy. Jesus promises that we will do even greater works than He did!

The Bible says that seeing God do the impossible should be a regular occurrence. Of course, there is dissonance at that statement because it does not conform with our experience. That is because of our narrow definition of the miraculous as only an instantaneous, inexplicable, and direct show of God's divine power. With that narrow definition, I haven't seen many miracles in my lifetime at all. You haven't either.

But if we expand our definition to include how God uses His people and His processes to accomplish the impossible, then we are living in truly miraculous times. If I allow myself to accept this broader understanding of miracles, then I am a miracle. You are one too.

You experienced a miracle when God helped you overcome the negative and harmful environment of your childhood. You experienced God's resurrection power when you broke free from the chains of addiction. You experienced the healing hands of Jesus when you learned to let go of your anger and forgive. You experienced the miracle of the fish and loaves when God multiplied your strength and compassion to love those who were hungry for love. You experienced the miracle of Jesus turning water into wine when He took your boring and ordinary life and gave you a story to tell from the mountaintops.

You see? You're a miracle. God has already done the impossible in your life. And He's not done yet.

This changes things, doesn't it? If God is still in the miracle working business then it's a whole new ball game. We should start to expect miracles. We should plan for miracles to occur. We should pray for God to send them and prepare to receive them. And we should participate in bringing them forth.

Here's my new definition:

A miracle is an act of God accomplishing the humanly impossible through the means of His divine power, His people, or His processes.

The 52-Day Miracle

Unconvinced? I want to show you an example of a bona fide God-honoring miracle. This was an act of God's providence and power. But it was not of the instantaneous variety. This miracle was achieved by a special group of people over a period of 52 days.

When you hear about this story, you might question if it would qualify as a miracle. I argue that it absolutely is a miracle because it could not have been done without God's direct intervention, guidance, provision, and protection.

The story I'm referring to is the story of Nehemiah rebuilding the wall of Jerusalem in 52 days. You're thinking, "How is that a miracle? That story seems so ordinary."

That's exactly the point. If you cannot see the miraculous power and presence of God throughout Nehemiah's story, you won't be able to see it your life today. Let's take a closer look at Nehemiah's story.

Nehemiah lived during a dark time in Israel's history. He was born in what is known as the Babylonian Captivity. In the year 586 BC, Jerusalem was attacked by the mighty Babylonian Empire. The city was besieged. The Temple was destroyed. The city burned to the ground. The inhabitants of Jerusalem were either killed or taken as slaves to Babylon.

Seventy years after the destruction of Jerusalem, the Babylonian Empire was overthrown by the Persian Empire. The Persians then allowed the Israelites to return to their homeland to begin to rebuild. Slowly the dispersed Israelites came home but they found everything a mess. Foreigners took over their land and claimed squatter's rights. And the Holy City still lay in ruins.

After many years, the Prophet Ezra led the people to begin a rebuilding project of the Temple. The Israelites became hopeful. And word begins to spread that Jerusalem was finally being rebuilt.

Nehemiah is an Israelite, but he had never seen Israel with his own eyes. He was born in Persia and was the personal servant of King Artaxerxes, son of Xerxes the Great. Xerxes the Great conquered most the known world and was featured in the movie *300* about the brave Greek warriors from Sparta.

Nehemiah was "cup-bearer to the king," which meant he was the king's personal bartender and tasted his food to make sure it wasn't poisonous. It had been twelve hopeful years since Ezra's repatriation and rebuilding project in Jerusalem began. One of Nehemiah's brothers visited Jerusalem to see the newly rebuilt Holy City for himself. When he came back, Nehemiah inquired about the progress of Jerusalem.

"Brother, tell me." Nehemiah asked, "How is the Holy City? Is it beautiful?"

"Nehemiah, you wouldn't believe it," his brother replied, "The place is a complete mess. The walls are broken down. The city is still in ruins. The people live in fear. There is no leadership or organization. It's a complete mess."

This is the setting of the 52-Day Miracle. The miracle of the story of Nehemiah is how God used him to do something that everyone thought was impossible. He would rebuild the walls that have been broken down for 140 years. And he would do it in only 52 days. *God reeely knows how to redeem time.*

[margin: ★ God's job / Our job]

There were so many pieces of the puzzle that had to fit together perfectly for him to succeed. God guided, protected, and provided for him every step of the way. I love this story because it seems so ordinary on the surface. It's essentially a building project. It's about good leadership, a simple plan, and focused determination. But that's what makes this story so great. Because is not God just as glorified by Nehemiah's wall as by giving sight to the blind, or turning water into wine? Is the rebuilding of Jerusalem also not the direct result of God's power and presence?

This qualifies as a miracle in my book. But this miracle was achieved through people and process. It took Nehemiah intentionality, planning, and focused effort for 52 consecutive days to accomplish this miracle.

I'm looking for these types of miracles in my own life. I'm looking for ways God could use me to bring Him glory by accomplishing the impossible through my intentional effort and obedience. The miraculous things that I've seen God do in my life were usually the ones that He asked me to participate in.

Nehemiah's story is an example and an inspiration for us. The breakthroughs and miracles that we are going to see in our lives are most likely the wall-building kind, not the water-into-wine variety. <u>We will see God use people and process far more frequently than the instantaneous demonstration of His power.</u> He wants to help you rebuild your marriage, resurrect your faith, and multiply your resources.

So how did Nehemiah go about accomplishing this miracle? I want to give you a summary of the process that Nehemiah took to accomplish his 52-day miracle.

Nehemiah took five steps to accomplish this miracle in 52 days. I think we can learn a lot from his example.

Step 1 - Receive and Clarify the Vision

After his brother came back from Jerusalem with the report that the city was still in ruins, Nehemiah's heart was broken. The Bible says he wept and mourned for days. This problem moved him so much that he dedicated a season for fasting and prayer. It was during this time he received a clear calling from God to rebuild the walls of Jerusalem.

- He received his assignment from God during his time of prayer and fasting.

What is God's assignment for you? You really need to figure this one out. This is where your miracles begin. It starts with being moved by the things that move God's heart. Vision usually starts by identifying a problem that God wants to be solved. (We'll talk more about vision in Chapter 5.)

The reason I planted the church I'm now leading began in a similar way. I was overwhelmed by the need of the lost people in my community. I live in one of the least-reached communities in America and God gave me the assignment of starting churches to reach them.

What problem has God brought to your attention? Perhaps within that problem is the seed of your calling and assignment.

Step 2 - Make a Simple Plan

Even though Nehemiah was a spiritual person, he was also a practical guy. While he was praying and fasting, he was also making a plan. It wasn't a complex plan. It was more of napkin doodle than a blueprint. But he had a plan.

When he got the chance, he presented this simple plan to the king. He didn't know the full details of what was needed to complete the project, but that didn't stop him from presenting his simple plan to his boss. He requested time off, a line of credit at the lumber yard, and some men to go with him. With that simple napkin plan, he set off to a place he had never been before to do something everyone thought impossible. He set off to honor God by attempting the impossible, to rebuild the walls of the Holy City that has been destroyed for 140 years.

Nehemiah had a clear and simple plan. It wasn't a detailed plan, but it was enough to get him started. You want to see God work in your life, but do you have a plan? If not, the second half of this book will show you how to create a simple plan to follow.

Step 3 - Start Small

When Nehemiah got to Jerusalem, he began by inspecting the wall. Then he gathered the people to explain his vision and plan of rebuilding the walls of Jerusalem. He instructed the people to begin with the small step of cleaning up their front yard and fixing the portion of the wall in front of their own homes.

It was a small beginning, but you have to start

small if you want to accomplish something big. The people got to work. Slowly, but surely, the work began.

Sometimes the reason we quit is that we are trying to do too much. We think we can complete the assignment in one day. This leaves us discouraged and exhausted. We need to learn the wisdom of starting small. How do you eat an elephant? One small bite at a time.

Nehemiah did what my mentor Bill Wellons often suggests by his aphorism: *Start small. Go deep. Dream big.*

Step 4 - Focus on the Work

It is so easy to get distracted from our primary assignment from God. We pursue the many good things instead of focusing on the one great thing God sent us to do. Shiny new objects compete for our attention. If we are going to fulfill our calling, we need to stay focused on the work.

Nehemiah faced constant distractions. He had many critics and enemies who did not want him to complete this project. Day after day, his critics invited him to join them in planning meetings.

"Let's meet for coffee and discuss this rebuilding project," they suggested. They constantly badgered him with these requests. His answer was the same each time:

> *I am doing a great work and I cannot come down. Why should the work stop while I leave it and come down to you?*

I love that statement. I've adopted Nehemiah's words to combat my own tendency to be distracted. When I am doing what I know I should be doing, shiny new objects, mental squirrels, and chaos monkeys try to distract me from my work. I speak Nehemiah's words out loud:

> *I am doing a great work and I cannot come down.*

Just repeating those words help nullify my distractions so I can focus on the work. If you're doing what God called you to do, don't allow distractions to get in the way. Focus on the work.

Step 5 - Overcome Obstacles

On your way to finding and fulfilling your assignment, you are going to encounter lots of obstacles. Each obstacle you encounter opportunity for you to quit and go home.

Nehemiah faced many obstacles on his path to fulfilling God's assignment for his life. God wanted him to rebuild the wall of Jerusalem. There were lots of obstacles along the way. He had never been to Jerusalem. He was born in Persia and had a demanding job serving the king. Many miles and preexisting commitments stood in his way. He also faced the obstacle of gathering the necessary resources and rallying the discouraged people of Jerusalem to help him do the work. When he arrived in Jerusalem, he discovered he had powerful enemies that stood in opposition to his plans to restore Jerusalem.

Nehemiah's critics and enemies did everything in their power to stand in his way. They used every possible means to get Nehemiah to stop. They used criticism, threats of physical harm, and conspiracy. But none of these tactics worked. Nehemiah overcame every obstacle and kept on building the wall until it was completed 52 days later.

I should warn you about something. Perhaps, you already know this. The greatest obstacle you will ever face is yourself. It's the internal obstacles, not the external ones, that will make you quit. That person who stares back at you in the mirror is often your greatest critic. Don't listen to him or her.

The greatest obstacles that you face come from inside your own head. It is much more difficult to overcome your own accusing thoughts about yourself than something someone else may say about you. The negative thoughts and words you tell yourself are so much more harmful because since they are already inside you, you're more likely to believe them. These harmful thoughts somehow got past your defenses and entered by some Trojan Horse during childhood, and are actively working against you.

My inner critic whispers (and sometimes screams) hurtful words of accusation into my ear every time I try to follow God's calling for my life. My critic has seen every one of my failures and he knows my deepest insecurities and uses them deftly against me.

His words cut deep into my soul.
- Who do you think you are?
- Do you think you're someone special?
- Do you really think God is going to use YOU?
- You're never going to change. Just give up. It won't work.
- What is everyone going to say about you?
- What if you fail?

- Come on. Think it over. It's not worth all the hard work.
- Why are you even doing this? You know you're going to quit again anyway.
- What if God lets you down and doesn't show up? Can you really trust Him?

My inner critic is so deceitful because he poses as an expert with my best interest in mind. But in truth, he is just a frightened and faithless child seeking comfort and security.

In those times, I must lovingly tell him, "I know you're scared. But we're doing a great work and we cannot come down." You must do the same to silence your inner critic.

Summary:

Nehemiah used these five simple steps to complete the wall of Jerusalem in only 52 days. This led to a national revival where all the people turned back to God. After the wall was rebuilt, the Israelites that were dispersed among the nations during the Babylonian exile began to return home to repatriate the Promised Land. Within a few years, Jerusalem was fully restored as a thriving metropolis and the center of worship and community for God's people.

It was a miracle.

This miracle wasn't achieved by an act of God's instantaneous power but by a person with an intentional plan. He had a simple plan and he worked that plan, and God used him in a great way.

I believe one of the reasons we don't see God's powerful hand at work in our lives today is because we are looking for the wrong type of miracles. We are waiting for the instantaneous water-into-wine miracles where we passively watch God do His thing. Those miracles are rare. But we need to realize the 52-Day Miracles are always available to us.

If God could use Nehemiah to do the impossible and rebuild something that had been broken for 140 years, and do it in only 52 days, what could God do in your life? What area of your life is God calling you to rebuild? Perhaps God is asking you to rebuild your marriage, or your faith, or your character.

In the next section, I will explain in detail how you can achieve this by using the *LIFE Path*. I believe these concepts have the power to change your life. I know this to be true because they have changed my life. The *LIFE Path* has helped me overcome major obstacles and grow in character, improve my marriage, and achieve my goals in life.

I have taught these concepts to hundreds of

people and have seen amazing results. The *LIFE Path* is a system that can become a powerful catalyst to help you experience personal breakthroughs in your life. But for it to be effective, you must follow the system.

CHAPTER 4

The Path Principle

***

The Hero's Journey

Can you guess the movie from these following scenes?

- *Scene 1 – He/She is an average person*
- *Scene 2 – He/She has a big problem*
- *Scene 3 – He/She meets a guide (or discovers a path)*
- *Scene 4 – He/She goes on a difficult journey*
- *Scene 5 – He/She confronts the problem*
- *Scene 6 – He/She becomes a hero*
- *Scene 7 – He/She returns home a new person*

Well, what movie is this story from? Who is our hero? If you guessed Luke Skywalker, Harry Potter, Frodo Baggins, Captain America, Batman, Rocky, The Karate Kid, Marty McFly, Katniss Everdeen, or Neo from *The Matrix*, you would be correct.

Have you ever noticed how the stories we love are all the same? My wife gets annoyed every time I point this out when we see a movie together.

"Shhh! You talk too much. Just let me watch the movie!" she tells me.

Sociologist Joseph Campbell calls this story structure *The Hero's Journey*. And it doesn't only apply to wizards, hobbits, and superheroes. These are also the stories of the men and women who line the Hall of Faith in the Bible. This is the story of Moses, Joshua, David, Gideon, Samuel, Elijah, Elisha, Esther, and many others.

The Hero's Journey is also our story, yours and mine. There's something innate about these stories that resonates in our hearts. We love to read and watch these stories because they ring in our souls and inspire us.

I'm a huge movie buff. My best advice is never get involved in a land war in Asia, never go against a Sicilian when death is on the line, and never challenge me in Hollywood Trivial Pursuit.

One of my favorite scenes in movies, especially from the glorious decade of the 80s, is what the screenwriters call the *fun and games* scene, or the *training montage*.

This is where Mr. Miyagi teaches Daniel-San karate by making him do Extreme Makeover: Home Edition on that little house in Reseda. This is the scene where Rocky goes *Eye of the Tiger* on those sides of beef and runs up the stairs in downtown Philly. This is where Bruce Wayne gets trained by Ra's Al Ghul, Luke learns to use the Force, and Morpheus teaches Neo how to kick butt in *The Matrix*.

You can usually spot the training montage scene by the totally awesome soundtrack where our heroes rock out to *Eye of the Tiger* in Rocky II, *You're the Best Around* in The Karate Kid, *It's the Power of Love* in Back to the Future, or even *Let's Hear it for the Boy* in Footloose. (By the way, in case you were wondering, the most awesome training montage ever made is in the classic 70s Kung Fu movie called *The 36th Chamber of Shaolin*. You're welcome.)

Okay, so you're probably wondering, "What does any of this have to do with me?"

Patience, Daniel-San. Just sand the floor. We are just beginning our journey together. There is an intentional path that I need to help you discover. You are beginning your hero's journey. Just as each of the heroes in those stories needed a guide or mentor to help them accomplish their mission, I want to help guide you to accomplish yours.

You've just met your mentor and now we are preparing you for the difficult journey you need to go on. You are at the bottom of the mountain, and you want to get to the top. So how do we get you from where you are to where you want to go? You follow the path, of course. The path that I'm going to show you is one that is simple to understand, but it will be difficult to implement.

The Path Principle

Years ago, I was taught to use a helpful tool called Life Planning. This is what my coach Brian Howard taught me many moons ago. Michael Hyatt also has a very helpful book on creating a life plan called *Living Forward*. A Life Plan is a useful tool that helps you determine your priorities, articulate your vision, and set short and long-range goals for yourself.

Life Planning has been helpful to me for many years, but I have made changes and additions to the process. The primary reason I made these changes is that I've come to dislike plans altogether. I dislike plans, especially complex ones because nothing ever goes according to plan! In the past, I've worked very hard to create an updated Life Plan document with 6 month and 3-year goals. Then within only a few weeks, life changes and these specific, measurable, action-oriented, realistic, and time-based goals no longer apply.

Life is often too unpredictable for plans. Of course, having any plan is better than having none. But if you are completely dependent on a specific plan, you're going to get yourself in trouble. Like Mike Tyson said, "Everyone has a plan until they get punched in the face."

So, what's better than a plan? Well, a path is infinitely better than a plan. A path is like the Yellow Brick Road that guided Dorothy and her friends to the Emerald City in the *Wizard of Oz*. In the following chapters, I'm going to show you how to use a system called *The LIFE Path*. It is like the Life Planning process but I believe it is far more practical and easier to follow. Perhaps the difference is just semantics and perspective. I guess a path is a type of plan, and a plan is a type of path. But seeing life as a path to follow and not a plan to implement has led to some major breakthroughs in my life.

Before we look at the specific elements of *The LIFE Path*, I want to spend a little time comparing the differences between a plan and a path. The reason I like the concept of a path is that I have a terrible sense of direction. I get lost a lot. It's gotten worse since I've become more and more dependent on GPS. Somehow smart technology has made me dumber. Of course, my wife reminds me that she is better at directions with her subtle eye rolls and the not so subtle, "Really? You're lost again?"

This usually leads to an argument because I'm an insecure person who needs to protect what little pride I have left. Honestly, I think she needs to give me a break. She doesn't struggle with being directionally-challenged. Somehow, she always gets where she wants to go. She doesn't even have to use the GPS. I think she was raised by Native American trackers who taught her how to interpret the shadows of the afternoon sun and navigate by the stars. It's not fair.

I wish she could have some empathy for my disability. There are two truths about getting lost that I wish she could one day understand.

One, I don't get lost on purpose. I really don't. I just think I'm smarter than Google Maps. I think there's a better route or shortcut that Google doesn't know about. But of course, every time I have disagreed with Google I've been wrong. It's amazing actually. How does Google always know the best route? It's uncanny. It's like they have satellites in space that monitor your position around the globe. Crazy, huh?

The second thing that I wish my wife knew about my condition is that I never actually know I'm getting lost until well after I've been lost for a while. When I am in the process of getting lost, I don't realize it. I'm driving confidently down the road thinking I know where I'm going. Only when I am many miles away from where I'm supposed to be, do I realize that I must have made a wrong turn 30 miles ago.

[Honey, if you're reading this. I just want to say, "You were right. I was wrong." There. Happy?]

Over a dozen years ago, I went to a conference for pastors and Christian leaders in Hotlanta. One of the speakers that spoke at the conference was Andy Stanley. I still remember that talk he gave because it really helped me come to grips with my problem about getting lost.

His message was called *The Path Principle*, which he later turned into a book with the same name. I recommend that book to you but I'll also summarize the main idea for you.

Pastor Stanley helped me figure out why I get lost so often, not only on the road but also in life. I've absorbed and internalized this principle into my life and I would like to share it with you but from my own perspective.

I grew up in Los Angeles. I love LA. It's the second largest city in our nation and it has everything. Great weather. Diversity. Amazing cultures from around the world. One of the things I love about Southern California is our geography. I cannot think of any other place on earth where you can watch the sunrise in the beautiful desert morning, go snowboarding in the mountains at lunch time, and go surfing and watch the sunset over the Pacific Ocean, all on the same day. These landscapes are only an hour or two away from each other by Freeway (that is, unless you get stuck in rush hour traffic, then it will take you two hours to go 5 miles).

Let's pretend I want to spend a day at the beach and go to Santa Monica. I tell the kids to put on their swim suits and gather the beach gear: boogie boards, sand toys, chairs, towels, cold drinks in the cooler, etc. Then I shepherd my little herd of cats into the minivan and channel the optimism of Clark Griswold on his quest to Wally World. Of course, I don't need to punch the coordinates in Google Maps because I grew up in LA. Everyone knows how to get to Santa Monica.

"Are you sure you know where you're going?" my loving wife asks.

"You don't think I know how to get to the beach?" I reply. "I grew up in SoCal. I know where I'm going. Ok?"

She foolishly decides to trust me and closes her eyes for a short nap and says, "Wake me up when we get to the beach."

The kids are arguing about something in the back. Kid #1 invaded kid #2's invisible bubble of sovereign personal space or something. I do my best to negotiate a peace treaty between the hostile parties by promising Happy Meals, all the while trying not to lose my salvation or cuss audibly.

In the process of the peace talks, I get on the on-ramp to the 10 Freeway. I was distracted by the kids and accidentally got on the 10 Freeway going East towards the mountains when I was supposed to go West towards the ocean. Honest mistake, right?

After 30-minutes of driving, I was expecting to see palms trees but instead, I start to see pine trees. Hmmm. Interesting. I start to wonder if I've taken a wrong turn somewhere.

The kids start asking, "Are we there yet?" I look up and, to my shock and horror, I see the foothills of the mountains. I consider covering my mistake by taking the kids to play in the snow instead. Maybe we could use the boogie boards as snow sleds. But then I realize they're only wearing swimsuits.

With no other option, I tap my wife on the shoulder, wake her up and meekly say, "Honey, I think we're lost again." (I want to point out this is a purely hypothetical story. I do get lost a lot, but not so bad as wanting to go to the beach and ending up in the mountains. I guess it helps that I live two miles away from the beach and I don't have to get on a freeway. However, once I did intend to go North to Hollywood and somehow ended up South in Orange County.)

What does this story have to do with your personal growth? Everything! Haven't you been paying attention?!

This is where Andy Stanley's *Path Principle* comes in. Here's the principle:

- *Your direction, not your intentions, will determine your destination.*

That's simple, right? It doesn't matter if I

intended to take my kids to the beach if I get on the freeway headed for the mountains. It doesn't matter how earnest and prepared I was to build sand castles and frolic in the waves, the route I chose brought me to my mountain destination.

The path that I chose determined my destination, regardless of my intentions.

This makes all the logical sense in the world when applied to geography and road maps. But the problem is we don't realize this principle also applies to life. For some reason, we believe that having hopes, dreams, and good intentions in life are enough to get us to our desired destination.

So many people get frustrated about where they ended up in life. They blame others and even get mad at God because their life is so different than what they hoped and dreamed it would be. They don't see the direct connection between the path they choose and their destination.

It's illogical, but so many people believe that their hopes, dreams, good intentions, enthusiastic effort, or even earnest prayers will somehow nullify or override the path they have chosen. It doesn't. The Path Principle always wins. Your direction, the path you choose, will determine your destination. Your hopes, best intentions, and prayer cannot override the path you've chosen.

Imagine how silly it would be for me to explain this to my wife.

"Honey, seriously. It's not my fault." I explain, "I intended to drive us to the beach!"

She would say, "I don't care about where you intended to go. What freeway did you get on?"

As obvious as this logic is when applied to SoCal freeways, we ignore how it applies to our life choices. You have already chosen many paths for your life. Each of these paths will lead to a specific and predetermined destination regardless of your intentions. You have already chosen a financial path. A relationship path. A career path. A character path. A family path. And especially a faith path.

Each of these paths will lead to a specific destination. This shouldn't surprise anyone, but somehow it always does.

For example, you hope and desire to have a godly spouse who loves Jesus. You imagine teaching Junior High Sunday School together and raising children to honor God. That's your intention. That's your dream. You've been praying for this since puberty. Perhaps you've even written it down in a Precious Moments journal. You diligently pray for God to send you Mr. or Ms. Right.

paths of life — there are many

Depending on your church background or denomination, you may even claim that blessing in the name of Jesus! You plead the blood of the Lamb. You draw prayer circles around that desire and claim that territory with all the confidence of Jabez himself.

You have good intentions for your future spouse. But none of that matters if you choose the path of singles' clubs, SnapChat flirting, and one-night stands. If the path you choose is chasing after the most attractive available person in the club, don't be surprised that you don't find the godly soulmate of your dreams. The problem wasn't your intentions. The problem was the path you chose.

You could apply the *Path Principle* to finances. Your intentions are to become financially wealthy, but you chose the path of overspending, and credit card debt. Don't be surprised that the path you've chosen will get you to your destination broke and in debt.

You intend to live for God and make a difference serving others. That's a great intention. But the path you've chosen is one of selfishness and greed. So, don't be surprised if you never make a difference for God. Remember, the path you choose that will determine your destination regardless of your intentions.

So be wise in choosing the right path. It's the path you choose that will get you to your destination. So, if you want to live a good life and leave a great legacy, ignore your intentions. Some say the road to hell is paved with good intentions. Make sure the path you're on will lead to the destination you want.

The thing I love about *The Path Principle* is that it is empowering. If you understand it, it frees you from being a powerless victim because it gives you choices. If you don't like where your life is now, don't sulk, blame, or complain. Just get off your current path and choose a new one, one that will lead towards the destination you want.

You don't have to stay on the bus if it's headed in the wrong direction. Now one is forcing you to stay on. Get off at the next stop and find a new path.

I believe thinking about personal growth as a path is so much easier and fun to follow than a life plan. I know, this is mainly a perspective change. But often a change of perspective makes all the difference.

Preview of the *LIFE Path*

In the following chapters, I will explain to you the system that I use to create my own *LIFE Path*. I've worked on this system for many years and have gotten it to a place where I believe it will be transferable and helpful to you.

Again, I want you to think of this tool as a path that you take as you make the journey to your preferred future destination. For any path to be useful, it should have at least two characteristics. One, it needs to take us where we want to go. Two, the path should be easy to follow with clearly marked out boundaries so we don't get off course.

This is also true with our *LIFE Path*. We need to have both a predictable destination and clear boundaries along the way. This is where the acronym of *LIFE* comes in. *LIFE* refers to the four basic elements of our path. There will be a chapter devoted to each of these elements. But here is a preview of *The LIFE Path*:

L = Legacy
I = Intentionality
F = Focus
E = Execution

These are the four irreducible components of the *LIFE Path*. They form the destination and the boundaries. *Legacy* refers to your preferred destination. This is where you want to get to. This is your mountaintop. In Chapter 5, I'll show you why the legacy of your relationships is so much more important than your list of accomplishments. I guarantee that if you follow my advice, you will be more motivated than ever to pursue a life that leaves behind a great legacy. Seriously, this section on legacy alone is worth the price of admission. It just might change your life.

Chapters 6 and 7 will be on *Intentionality* and *Focus*. These two represent the guardrails and boundaries that keep you on your path. These two concepts will keep you from wandering and drifting. Personally, applying these two concepts has radically changed my life.

Chapter 8 is on *Execution*. No, I'm not talking about murder or capital punishment. I'm referring to the successful implementation of a plan or idea. We're going to get extremely practical. I'm going to give you helpful tips and hacks to improve your productivity and change your mindset so that you can create helpful habits.

So, Daniel-San, I have a lot to teach you. If you're ready to get started, sand the floor. Wax on. Wax off. Let's get to work.

CHAPTER 5

L is for Legacy

***

Alfred's Legacy

Alfred was given a rare gift. He got to read his own obituary with enough opportunity to change it. He was a scientist and inventor. He was the Tony Stark of his day. No, he wasn't Iron-Man. But he was a genius inventor who became ultra rich by developing weapons for the military. During the height of his business, he owned over ninety factories that produced bombs, grenades, and other weapons of war.

One day he was given an unusual gift that

changed the course of his life and his legacy forever. He was a real-life Ebenezer Scrooge who got a second chance after being visited by Marley's three ghost friends. Alfred was one of the few people who got to hear what people would say about him after he died while he was still living. While he was out of the country on a business trip, his brother died. The newspaper somehow got the information wrong and printed an obituary and article about Alfred.

The title of the article read "The Merchant of Death Has Died." It described Alfred as the man who "became rich by finding ways to kill more people faster than ever before." The newspaper editor seemed to be glad the world was rid of his greedy villainy.

When Alfred read that article, it changed the trajectory of his life. He knew that if he didn't change, his legacy would be one of greed, war, and death. He vowed to change his legacy. He decided to give away 94% of his vast wealth to create an endowment that would award prizes to people who promoted the cause of peace and humanity around the world.

This is the story of Alfred Nobel. Nobel wanted to change his legacy. He didn't want his name to be associated with war and death. But rather he wanted his name associated with education, the arts, and mostly peace. Today, when we hear the name of Alfred Nobel, we don't think of "The Merchant of Death." We think of the highest honor an individual can receive, the Nobel Peace Prize. Past recipients of this award are among the most significant people in the modern era, such as Gandhi, Mother Teresa, Martin Luther King Jr., and Nelson Mandela.

Most people don't think much about their legacy, especially not young people. But thinking about your legacy could be one of the most beneficial and motivational activities you could do. This was the case for Alfred Nobel. Thinking about his legacy changed the trajectory of his life.

The Importance of Legacy

What about you? What if you could peer into the future and see your legacy? Would that change how you lived today? Would it cause you to change your current trajectory?

Let's talk about your legacy. What is it? Why is it important? How can you build a great one?

There are three core concepts regarding legacy that I want you to know.

1) Your legacy is everything you leave behind after you die.

I've never seen a hearse pulling a U-Haul. You can't take anything with you after you die. You have to leave it all behind. And the sum total of whatever it is that you leave behind is your legacy.

A legacy can simply be defined as something handed down from one generation to the next. When most people think about leaving something for the next generation, they think about leaving an inheritance of property or riches to their loved ones.

Well, that is one type of legacy. But there are other types of legacies you can leave behind. You can leave behind a legacy of faith, of love, impact, and great memories with family. Your legacy could be measured by the impact you've made in the lives of the people closest to you.

2) The legacy of your relationships is more important than your accomplishments.

Just imagine that you are a wildly successful business person. You made millions. Created companies. Did well with your financial investments. You have amassed a surplus of wealth that will take care of the next several generations of descendants. You've made it! That's the American Dream, right?

Then what? What's next? One of the highest honors given to a person is to have a building named after them. You see it when you visit a University or a new hospital. They usually have buildings named after people who made large donations to their organizations.

There's the John Wayne Cancer Institute in L.A. At the University I attended, there is a building called Sutherland Hall. I'm not sure who Mr. Sutherland was, but I bet he made a big donation to the school to get his name on the building. (Perhaps it was Keifer Sutherland. Maybe not. I couldn't imagine Jack Bauer attending Bible College.)

What does worldly success give you? If you're lucky, you could get your name on a building. That honor represents the height of earthly success.

You can focus all your energy to attain that legacy, or you can focus on the legacy of your relationships. I believe that the legacy of your relationships is so much more important than your success. Your character and relationships represent what Stephen Covey calls "Primary Greatness." Worldly and financial success is the "Secondary Greatness" that comes from the primary greatness of your character and relationships.

If you only pursue the secondary greatness of success, your focus will be on building a good resume. You want to be able to look good on that piece of paper and show a track record of success and experience to future employers.

So many young people are obsessed with building a good resume. It starts in High School, or even before. Students are so concerned with their scores on the SAT, ACT, GPA, AP and other alphabet soup measurements. Most students also invest their time in extracurricular activities such as sports, music, clubs, and student leadership to look good to college recruiters. This resume building focus continues throughout college. Then it's the corporate ladder. Climb baby, climb!

But for what? Even if you are wildly successful in your career, the best you can hope for is to have your name on the side of a building one day. Sounds like the ladder you've been climbing is leaning on the wrong building.

I know what you're thinking. You want to ask, "If I shouldn't try to build a good resume, what should I focus on?" Great question. I'm glad you asked. That's the million-dollar question.

Here's my answer. It might surprise you:

Don't live for your resume. Live for your eulogy.

A eulogy is what they will say about you at your

funeral. It literally means the "good words" spoken about you at your memorial service. I am convinced that a eulogy is the best measurement of a good legacy. How the people closest to you will remember you is the most important thing about your life.

You need to stop building your resume and focus on building your eulogy. As Jesus asked, "What good is it to gain the world and lose your soul?" What good is it to have a building named after you, if you've made zero positive impact in the lives of those around you?

If you want to build your legacy you need to shift the focus from building your resume to building your character and your relationships. Those are the two essential elements of a great legacy. Your character. Your relationships.

Now God may have some big plans to use you in some great global way. God's plan for your life may include great accomplishments and international influence. His plan for you might be bigger than just your character and your relationships. True. But, listen up. God's plan for you may be more than your character and relationships but it is not less than that. God's plan for your life begins with your character and relationships as the foundation.

I hope this doesn't sound like a sick confession

but I enjoy going to funerals. Being a pastor, I've attended more than most. I enjoy funerals ten-times more than weddings. The hopeful naïveté of young love on display at weddings is annoying. It's cute, but that guy in the rented tux has no idea what it means to love someone in sickness or in health. He is just mouthing optimistic words he knows nothing about. I'll take a good funeral over a wedding any day.

Ecclesiastes 7:1-2 says,
A good name is better than precious ointment,
and the day of death than the day of birth.
It is better to go to the house of mourning
than to go to the house of feasting...

Weddings are forward-looking, but funerals reflect on the past. In my opinion, there is nothing more encouraging and inspiring than attending the funeral of a Christian person who loved and served Jesus and the people in his life well. Earlier this year, I got the privilege to attend the funeral of the father of a good friend. Clayton was a godly Christian businessman who was faithful in loving his family and serving his church. His widow, children, grandkids, pastor, and friends lined up to share how he impacted their lives. Clayton's legacy was etched, not on the side of a building, but on the lives of every person who knew him.

That funeral service was more honoring to God and inspirational than any church service I ever attended. Even the unbelievers in attendance felt the presence of God. (Note: the unbelievers were given a book on heaven with a letter from the pastor explaining the Gospel. It was Clayton's idea.)

So, if you are interested, let me tell you how you can begin building a great legacy. This leads us to the next core concept about legacy.

3) The wisest thing you can do is to plan your funeral.

Psalm 90 says "Teach us to number our days, that we may gain a heart of wisdom." Wisdom comes from acknowledging the scarcity of days we have on earth and becoming faithful stewards of the time we have left. Ann Lamott reminds us that it is good to live as though we are dying. Because we are. Our time on earth is not unlimited. It's finite. How will you spend it?

So, I want to help you plan your funeral. Not really. But I do want you to think about the legacy that you are leaving behind, and thinking about your funeral helps.

Planning Your Funeral

I want to show you four steps to strengthening your legacy. You will want to revisit these steps and make adjustments and edit it along the way. Here are four steps I use to help me build a worthy legacy. I'll also give you my personal legacy statements as an example.

Step 1 - Make a list of the significant people in your life.

Who will be at your funeral? Think about the people who are important to you. These are the people that you really care about. On average, a person has eight to fifteen significant and close relationships. You can have more or less than that. Who are they? Write down their names. Just brainstorm the names of people that you care about.

Go ahead. Make that list. This is the first step. We can't go to step two until you do this.

Step 2 - Group and prioritize your relationships.

Now take the list of names that you wrote down in Step One and put them into groups. Some are family, others are friends, co-workers, church members, or golfing buddies. Categorize your relationships.

These are the different relationship accounts you have in your life. These groups of people define who you are because you play a different role in each of these relationships. You are a spouse, parent, child, sibling, friend, co-worker, boss, neighbor, etc. As you write down your relationships, don't forget two of the most important relationships you have. Your relationship with God and your relationship with yourself.

Now that you made a list of your relationships, I want you to prioritize these relationships. Place them in the order of focus, not necessarily in the order of importance. The relationships at the top should be the ones that need the most attention from you now.

Here's my prioritized list of relationships:
1. My wife
2. Myself
3. Church Leaders
4. Congregation
5. My family and friends
6. My children
7. God

If you notice, my children and God are at the bottom of my list. Why is that? That's not because they are less important than my other relationships. In fact, my relationship with God and my three children are among the most important things in my life. The reason that they are at the bottom of the list is that I'm doing good in these relationships right now. Even though they occasionally make me go coo-coo for cocoa puffs, I have a good relationship with my kids. And my spiritual life is as strong as its been in years.

However, at the top of my list is my relationship with my wife and my relationship with myself. My wife and I have just completed (hopefully) the two most difficult years of our marriage. We became caretakers for my angry, alcoholic, and terminally-ill mother. She lived with us for a year and a half before she died.

Although God redeemed the situation by helping me resolve some deep childhood wounds and having my mom come to faith in Jesus three months before she died, it was a long trial. The whole experience was completely soul-draining and hard on my marriage. We've decided to seek professional counseling to help us work through these issues. That's why my marriage is in the #1 position of priority. It's because that is my primary area of focus at this moment.

Step 3 - How do you want them to remember you?

Now that you have a prioritized list of relationships, I want you to answer this question for each group:

How do I want [insert name of group] to remember me?

This is not going to be easy. For many, this is the most difficult part of the *LIFE Path*. Emotions often overwhelm people when they attempt this. I cry like a preteen girl at a Bieber concert every time I revise my *LIFE Path*.

One by one, take each relationship account and write out what you would like them to remember about you. How do you want your spouse to remember you? How do you want your kids to remember you? If you are a boss, how do you want your employees to remember you? If you're a pastor, how do you want your congregation to remember you?

Again, imagine your funeral. The preacher is going to be formal and polite. But what are your buddies and those closest to you going to say about you as they grab a coffee or drive to the cemetery? What do you hope that they would say about you?

For each relationship group, follow this prompt:

I want [insert name of group] to remember that I _____.

Here's how I want my wife to remember me:

I want Kerry to remember that she was the love of my life. That she was the best thing that (outside of Jesus) ever happened to me. She was an absolute gift from God to me.

I want her to remember that I only had eyes for her and was absolutely in love with her. I want her to remember how committed I was in providing for her and our family and that I knew and understood and cared for her.

I want her to remember how we grew to love each other more and more. That I loved her and served her as best I could. That I was intentional in growing to become the man that she needs me to be. That I tried very hard to become a good listener who was caring, compassionate, and patient because that was what she needed me to be.

I want her to remember that I worked hard to make our family a priority and provided a safe home environment so that we all could thrive.

I want Kerry to remember that we were great partners in life and ministry. We worked hard to figure out our differences and learned to appreciate them. I want her to remember that I was honored to be her husband and that she was so special to me.

I want Kerry to remember that I thought she was the most amazing person in the world. That I was thankful and grateful for who she is and all the sacrifices she made to love me, our children, and others around us, especially my mom and family.

I want her to remember that I was intentionally romantic, funny, caring, and passionate. She was my best friend and I loved spending time with her going on walks and talking.

I want her to remember that even with all our trials and difficulties, we really enjoyed raising kids, mentoring others, starting churches, and doing life together. That I thought she was one of the most gifted servants of Christ there is. That I fully believed in her and supported her completely.

I want her to remember that I took time and intentional steps to know her heart and love her the way she needed to be loved. That I was her best friend and she could tell me anything. That I was a good listener. That I made her feel safe and helped her thrive in life. That I was fully present with her and that she was my priority. That I absolutely treasured her because she made my life better in every way.

I know that was long. It's repetitious, full of grammatical errors, and run-on sentences. But to me, it's meaningful. It didn't edit it much when I wrote it. I just let my emotions flow.

When you write, don't self-edit. Just come up with a terrible first draft. It's okay. You don't have to even show it to anyone. In fact, my wife never saw this before I wrote it here in this book. The only people that I showed this to were a few guys who were my accountability partners.

Here's how I want my children to remember me:

I want my children, Stephen, Emily, and Elizabeth to remember that I loved them with all my heart and they were the joy of my life. I want them to remember that I was present and involved in their lives and I cared about each of them individually.

I want them to remember that I loved Jesus and serving the Church with so much passion that they also made Jesus and the Church their passion too. I want them to be able to point back to me and their mom as the reason they love Jesus and the Church so much.

I want them to remember that I saw each of them as a special, unique, and amazing gift from God and they each made me exceptionally proud to be their father.

I want them to look back at their confidence, courage, love, generosity, work ethic, successful life, accomplishments, strong family, and world impact and point to the seeds of faith and vision I planted in their hearts when they were young.

I want them to remember that our family time together was a top priority. Dinner together was a special time that was valued and protected.

I want them to remember that I was absolutely in love with and committed to their mom.

I want them to remember family vacations, new adventures, and their personal "daddy days" with me.

I want them to remember that I believed in them unconditionally and that helped lay the foundation for their humble, yet powerful sense of self-confidence.

I want them to remember that they were important to me, and I was always available for them and what I was a patient and good listener. That they could always talk to me about their problems and fears. That I quickly admitted my mistakes and asked for forgiveness.

I want them to remember and treasure our family times together so much that we all committed to staying close and have regular family dinners and vacations together even after they grew up.

I want them to remember that I lived what I preached. That I knew I wasn't perfect, but I was genuine, humble, and intentional. I was intentional in teaching them and preparing them for life. That I was their example that helped them become hard workers, innovative, and successful in their lives. That I helped them become good with money and modeled how to live with faith and generosity.

I want them to remember that I believed in them and thought they were special. That they were gifts given to me from God. I want them to remember the hugs, smiles, laughter, food, partnership in marriage, love for Jesus, and the value of serving others and generosity. That my example is an inspiration and a guide for them. That I set them up to thrive and be successful in life and relationships.

I want them to remember that I modeled well for them a genuine Christian life. That my love and my commitment to Jesus and the Church was a result of my understanding and gratitude for the Gospel. That I believed that God is good, loving, wise, and strong and deserved our complete trust.

I want them to remember that I thought their mom was the most amazing person in the world. And Jesus was worth leaving everything to follow and the Church is worth serving. And that God has a plan for each of them and wants to use them to change the world.

I cried when I originally wrote these two sections.

That's because many of these aspirations are not true yet. But just writing them down calls me to a higher level of commitment. It inspires me to be a better man.

This will most likely be the longest section of your *LIFE Path*. This section may be difficult for you to write. It is for many people. But let me give you a tip that will get you started in the right direction. Start with the easiest group first. Don't start with your spouse or your children. Start with your co-workers or your business partners. Every time I revise the section on my wife and kids, I get emotional. So, I don't begin there. I ease into it.

Step 4 - Write your eulogy.

Just imagine that you live to the ripe old age of 100 and you have accomplished everything you wanted to accomplish and more. Then you pass away painlessly in your sleep. Every person that you love is still alive. They are gathered together in a church sanctuary with stained glass and dark wooden pews. They are there to remember, celebrate and honor your life. You lived your life with purpose and you finished well.

The preacher gets up to the pulpit and opens the service with a prayer and words of welcome. Then your best friend nervously walks up to the lectern. He unfolds a piece of paper with shaky hands, clears his throat. Then begins to read your eulogy. Your whole life is about to be summarized in a few short paragraphs.

What do you want your best friend to read at your funeral? What's written on your eulogy? Do you want it to list your many accomplishments and success? Do you want it to describe your wealth and collection of toys and trinkets? At this point, do any of those things even matter? It seems that the things that the world uses to measure success cease to hold much value on the day of your funeral.

It's your turn to write out your eulogy. Take what you've written from the previous section about how you want to be remembered and start there. This will feel awkward, but the process will inspire you. I continue to read parts of the eulogy that I've written for myself each morning. It has a way of helping me focus on what's important and keeping me motivated.

As you write your eulogy, write it in the third person, past tense. Place yourself in the position of your best friend. Write it as if you were an outside witness to your life. Describe it as best you can.

Here's the eulogy that I want to be read at my funeral:

Thien was a person whose life made an impact on the lives of all who knew him and to many thousands of others who were touched by his ministry. Thien was a pastor, author, ministry leader, husband, father, friend, uncle, and grandfather.

He lived his life with the clear goal of "changing his world for Christ." He was committed to that goal and lived his life with intentionality in pursuit of that goal. In seeking to accomplish his life mission, Thien lived by a clear life philosophy that was made up of four commitments:

1) Take it personally. Whatever you do, do it with all your heart as unto the Lord.

2) Make it better. If it's worth doing, it's worth doing poorly the first time. But make sure you commit to improving.

3) Be intentional. You don't reach your goals by accident. You need to be intentional.

4) Ask for help. You can't do it by yourself. Be humble enough to ask for help.

Thien was a devoted follower of Jesus, having been changed by Jesus as a teenager. This was demonstrated by how he served Jesus with passion, joy, and gratitude. He spent over 50 years in ministry, having personally planted and pastored three local churches. He was used by God to help catalyze a church planting movement among Vietnamese Americans and among other people groups.

Thien was a prolific author, having written over 50 books, Bible Studies, and Leadership Curriculum. He trained, mentored, and coached pastors to be more effective in ministry. Through his speaking, teaching, writing, and the resources that he created, he has touched the lives of tens of thousands.

But his greatest love in ministry was Citylights Church, which he founded and pastored until his death. He was humbled and amazed and full of gratitude that God would use him to impact so many lives. The people of Citylights always knew that they had a pastor that loved God, the Scriptures, and loved them with all his heart. Half of the membership of Citylights came to faith under his ministry.

Thien is most proud of the over 20 pastors and church planters that he trained, mentored, and sent out. Thien helped them start over 20 daughter churches and 50 granddaughter churches. Through the ministry of Citylights Church, he has made a huge impact in the community through their church planting center, community center, thrift store, and other community-focused non-profit organizations.

But Thien's greatest legacy isn't the books, ministries, churches, or organizations that he started. It is his family. He leaves behind his lifelong love, Kerry, his bride of over 60 years. She remembers that he loved, served, cherished, cared for, believed in, and nurtured her throughout their marriage. He worked hard to be an understanding, caring, and compassionate husband. She felt loved and special. She remembers that he was always intentional in making her a priority. She loved that he led them to build a Christ-centered family with children who all love and serve Jesus.

Thien's three children, Stephen, Emily, and Elizabeth remember that their father was always present throughout their lives. He adored each child and somehow made them each feel that they were his favorite, each uniquely loved by him. They will always remember his humor, cooking, daddy dates, vacations, and how he loved and cared for their mom. He is their model and inspiration for their faith in Jesus. He was not a perfect person or father. He had his flaws and failures, but he was always ready to admit his faults and ask for forgiveness. They will remember his passion, generosity, commitment, and presence in their lives. He will be missed.

As I reread my own eulogy, I feel the need to tell you that only about 7% of these statements are true of me today. But this eulogy describes what I aspire to.

As you write out your eulogy, you need to silence your inner critic. You're going to hear an annoying and critical voice question, "Who do you think you are?" It could be the disembodied voice of your mom, your Frenemy, your 3rd Grade teacher, or your ex. Don't listen to those accusing and condemning voices. Ignore them.

This eulogy is not reality. Not yet. This is dream time. This is clouds, not dirt. Don't worry about sounding arrogant, prideful, or unrealistic. You don't even have to show anyone else this document. It's just for you. Go ahead and write a terrible and awkward first draft. It's okay. Give yourself permission to dream.

Summary

One of the most inspirational quotes I've ever read comes from Marianne Williamson, although it is falsely attributed to Nelson Mandela. It reads:

Our deepest fear is not that we are inadequate. Our deepest fear is that we are powerful beyond measure. It is our light, not our darkness that most frightens us. We ask ourselves, who am I to be brilliant, gorgeous, talented, and fabulous?

Actually, who are you not to be? You are a child of God. Your playing small does not serve the world. There is nothing enlightened about shrinking so that other people will not feel insecure around you.

We are all meant to shine, as children do. We were born to make manifest the glory of God that is within us. It is not just in some of us; it is in everyone and as we let our own light shine, we unconsciously give others permission to do the same. As we are liberated from our own fear, our presence automatically liberates others.

So, who are you not to be great? You are a child of the Most High King. Redeemed by the precious blood of Jesus. A temple of the Holy Spirit who resides in you. A masterpiece created in Christ Jesus for good works which God has prepared in advance for you to walk in. God has an amazing plan to use your life to bring Him glory and honor. Imagine what God can do through you if you really believed what the Bible says about you.

Silence your inner critic and write down your dreams. Let me help you get started. Answer this question:

> *If you were absolutely confident that God is with you, wants to bless you, and use you to bring Him glory, what would you like to accomplish in your lifetime?*

Answer that question. Start there. Then imagine living your life in a focused and intentional pursuit of that vision. Imagine living to 100 years old with the satisfaction and joy of accomplishing everything and more than you imagined possible to the glory of God.

Then write it down in your eulogy.

CHAPTER 6

I is for Intentionality

* * *

What is Intentionality?

The second component of the *LIFE Path* is *intentionality*. It acts as one of the two guardrails that keep you on the path to accomplishing your legacy. I cannot overstate the vital role that intentionality plays on your *LIFE Path*. I believe it is one of the primary keys to unlocking your potential.

What is *intentionality*? Let's try to define it. To be intentional is to do something on purpose. Intentionality is the opposite of accidental. It is the deliberate choices and actions you must take to accomplish your specific goals. It is the opposite of drifting.

When you are drifting through life, you are passively allowing life's currents take you wherever they please. Of course, drifters don't always end up in terrible places. Sometimes the winds take them to nice places. But drifters never make it to the top of the mountain. No one reaches the peak of Everest without intending to do so.

To create the great legacy you desire, you must reject your passivity. Being passive is so easy because it requires no work. Passivity is our enemy. It is the reason we drift through life as a rudderless raft.

Passive drifting can only take you down the stream of mediocrity where the masses are. You cannot reach the mountaintop by drifting down the river. Climbing to the top is hard. No wonder most people prefer to drift. The river is crowded by the easily entertained and satisfied masses. Don't be one of them.

This reminds me of the scene in the *Percy Jackson* movie about the Lotus Hotel. This is a modernized telling of the Lotus-Eaters story in Homer's Odyssey. Percy and friends had been lured away from their quest into the luxurious comfort of the Lotus Hotel and they didn't want to leave. They were given everything they wanted. Rich foods. Free entertainment. Unlimited video games. They started to become self-indulgent and placated teenage zombies. What began as only a brief rest stop stretched into five days before they realized it was more than a distraction. It was a trap. Later they learned that some of their friends had to be rescued from the Lotus Hotel after being trapped for five years in this luxurious self-indulgent prison.

Sometimes the most effective prisons are the fun and comfortable ones. Only intentional people, people on a quest, can escape the powerful tractor-beam of comfortable mediocrity. The legacy you aspire to cannot be found at the bottom of the lazy river. It's only found at the top of the mountain. The only way to get to the mountaintop is to reject the river of passivity and be intentional in finding and pursuing your *LIFE Path*.

The path to the top of the mountain is not easy. It's not supposed to be. You cannot passively drift your way there. But the good news is that the path is not crowded. Most of your peers are on life's lazy river. Intentionally pursuing your *LIFE Path* will set you apart from the pack.

Shakespeare's best play (IMHO), *The Twelfth Night* has this wonderful reoccurring line:

Some are born great.
Some achieve greatness.
And some have greatness thrust upon them.

Some are born great. That first line is about the privileged few who are born on third base. To score a run, all they have to do is not do anything stupid and wait for the next guy up to get a hit.

And some have greatness thrust upon them. That last line describes the few fortunate souls that fall into the lap of luck or win the lottery.

But the rest of us are represented by the potential of that second line: *Some achieve greatness.* Most of us are not born great and can't rely on winning the lottery. So, if greatness is something we want, we must be intentional in finding a way to achieve it ourselves.

Of the three, I believe this is the preferred position to be in. It's better to have to get your hustle on and figure out a way to achieve greatness. Only those who have gone through this experience can appreciate the journey to greatness. And they're the only ones who know how to get back there if they ever get lost.

Intentionality is essential on the *LIFE Path*. If you want to reach your destination, you must be purposeful and prepared. Anyone can be average. By definition, most people are. There are very few that enjoy the fullness of God's blessings in their lives and achieve a great legacy. Why not be one of them?

So many people have goals and dreams about the life they want. They can tell you where they want to live, what cars they'll own, where they'll go on family vacations with their 2.3 children. They may have a picture of the legacy they would like to leave behind. Some can describe the mountaintop to you in inspiring and breathtaking detail. But if you ask them how they are going to achieve this goal, they have no idea.

These people are *so heavenly minded that they are no earthly good*. If that describes you, then you have a problem with clouds and dirt. Clouds represent dreams, goals, and aspirations. Dirt represents the challenging work that you need to put in to achieve those dreams.

An intentional person must be good at both. He must have his head in the clouds and his hands in the dirt. Because a dream without a plan is just a wish. And a wish without a dream is just a task.

Intentional people are both dreamers and doers. Seth Godin says that the secret of the most successful innovators like Steve Jobs and Elon Musk is that they ship their products. They don't spend forever in research and development. They ship their products, sometimes even before it is completely ready. It doesn't matter how groundbreaking your product is, you can't sell it if you never ship it to market.

Intentionality is one of the guardrails on the *LIFE Path* that will keep you on course. So, let me show you how to build this guardrail. There are four steps.

Intentionality Step 1 - Take 100% Responsibility

We discussed the importance of taking responsibility in the chapter on prerequisites (remember the DVR?). I won't belabor the point too much. But let me ask you this question:

Who is responsible for achieving the legacy that you desire?

You considered how you want people to remember you and wrote out the eulogy that you hope will be read at your funeral. Now, who is responsible for making that a reality?

You are. It is 100% your responsibility to achieve your goals. It doesn't matter what obstacles are in your way or how many people have hurt you in the past. If you are going to achieve that dream, you must take complete responsibility for your life.

Stephen Covey says that the foundation of an effective person begins with being proactive and taking full responsibility for your choices. It is having the mindset that says, "I am fully responsible for me and I can choose."

Author Denis Waitley says that responsibility is a sign of maturity. He writes:

> *A sign of wisdom and maturity is when you come to terms with the realization that your decisions cause your rewards and consequences. You are responsible for your life and your ultimate success depends on the choices you make.*

No more excuses. Put on your big boy pants and take responsibility.

Intentionality Step 2 - Create your job descriptions

I take responsibility for my life by looking at the different areas of my life as jobs I need to accomplish. I have people working for me and I am their boss. I have to create job descriptions for every role in the organization I lead.

For these job descriptions to be useful, they must be simple and clear. They usually consist only of two or three paragraphs.

This is what I want you to do for the distinct roles in your life. For each relationship account you have, write out a job description for the role that you play in that relationship.

I play distinct roles in each of my different relationships. I wear different hats. I am a husband, a father, a pastor, a boss, a friend, a brother, an uncle, etc. Each of these roles demands different things from me.

Each job description should have at least two parts: a purpose statement and a vision description. A purpose statement defines your role in that relationship. And a vision description is a detailed explanation of what success looks like in that area of your life.

When writing your job descriptions, make sure you are writing in the present tense. Think "I am" instead of "I will."

Here are some examples of my job descriptions: (Notice that I threw in a Bible verse for inspiration because I'm an overachiever.)

[Life Account #1 – Christian]

Purpose: I am a follower of Jesus. My purpose is to pursue a growing relationship with Jesus exhibited by an increasing intimacy, trust, joy and gratitude.

Vision: *I am passionately pursuing a closer relationship with Jesus. I am growing to love, trust, and enjoy Him more each day. I am full of gratitude and joy because of my relationship with God.*

Quote: *"This is eternal life: that they may know you, the only true God." (John 17:3)*

[Life Account #2 – Husband]

Purpose: *My purpose is to love, care for, nurture, and help my wife thrive in her life.*

Vision: *I am in a fulfilling and satisfying marriage with my best friend. Kerry feels cared for, honored, cherished, secure, and loved. I am sensitive, caring and attentive to her needs. I show her love in her love language of daily "acts of service." I am her best friend and we have a close, intimate, secure, and fun relationship. Kerry is alive with joy and is thriving as a person.*

Quote: *"Husbands love your wives as Christ loved the church." (Ephesians 5:25)*

[Life Account #3 – Health]

Purpose: *My purpose is to take care of my body so I can have the energy to love my family and be effective at my calling to serve God and the Church.*

Vision: *I am in the best shape of my adult life. I have more than enough energy to keep up the with stresses and demands of life without getting tired or grumpy. I weigh 180 lbs. and live an active life with my children. We enjoy doing active things together as a family such as jogging, biking, and hiking.*

Quote: *"Do you not know that your body is the temple of the Holy Spirit who is in you, whom you have from God? You are not your own. For you were bought with a price. Therefore honor God with your body." (1 Cor. 6:19-20)*

Now it's your turn. Write out a job description for each of your relationship accounts. You don't have to follow exactly my format for creating your job description. The goal is for you to have clarity on your purpose and a clear vision that compels you to action.

Intentionality Step 3 - Assess your current reality

Now that you have a job description for every role that you are responsible for, you're ready for Step Three. To see if you are making progress, you must take an honest assessment of where you currently are. It is impossible to be in denial and still make intentional progress. The Bible refers to self-deluded people that are "so nearsighted that they are blind" (2 Peter 1:9). Don't be blind to your current reality.

We lie to ourselves and to others constantly. When someone asks us, "How are you doing?"

We instinctive say, "I'm fine." All the while knowing that we are anything but fine. We say, "I'm fine" so much that we start to believe our own propaganda and fake news.

Jim Collins, in his book *Good to Great*, says that the best leaders discipline themselves to confront the brutal facts of their current situation. They want the truth no matter how brutal it may be. No sugar coating. Just give it to me straight. They courageously seek to face and understand their circumstances honestly. But they do it with an unwavering determination and faith that no matter how bad the situation is, they can improve it.

This is not an easy step because it requires humility and taking responsibility for your failures and foolish choices. I mentioned earlier that my wife and I are seeing a counselor to help us work on our marriage. This has been the best thing for our marriage in this season. Initially, it was hard for me to admit we needed to pay a professional for this. When I humbled myself and took an honest assessment of how I was doing as a husband, I realized I needed help to work on this area.

Here's your assignment. For every area that you wrote a job description for, I want you to describe your current reality. While the job descriptions are aspirational and future oriented, the current reality must be current and brutally honest.

I know this can be a painful step for you. It was for me. But here is my honest assessment of my reality.

[Life Account #1 – Christian]
Current Reality:
- *I am doing good. I'm growing. But not very consistent or intentional with my personal devotions.*
- *My faith is sometimes mixed up with the ups and downs of ministry.*
- *I worry a lot about things that I should trust God for.*

[Life Account #2 – Husband]
Current Reality:
- *I'm often negative, angry, impatient, or not fully present.*

- *Kerry doesn't always feel safe to share her feelings and she is often defensive because of my reactions.*
- *She tells me that I don't help around the house enough.*

[Life Account #3 – Health]
Current Reality:
- *I weigh 208 lbs.*
- *I don't sleep well and have serious acid reflux issues.*
- *I get tired and grumpy and lose my patience with my family too often.*
- *My left knee and both ankles hurt. I can't play basketball or run without my injuries hurting. My cardio is terrible.*

When you write out your current reality, you must be brutally honest with yourself. Don't delude yourself into thinking that everything is great. But you must never lose hope that you can still make progress. You must have both a clear understanding of your challenges and optimistic resiliency to pursue improving these areas.

Intentionality Step 4 - Create Goals and Milestones

If you are hiking on a trail, you would look for milestones to see if you're still on the right path. Milestones or goals are essential to measuring your progress. Matt Mullenweg, the creator of WordPress, said in an interview, "You can't change what you don't measure." I agree. We need to create goals or milestones to measure our progress.

Goal-setting and creating milestones doesn't have to be complex. Let's be practical and keep it simple. There are only four types of goals that you can create:

1) Do more of something
2) Do less of something
3) Start something new
4) Stop doing something

That's it. It's either more, less, start or stop. Every goal you can possibly conjure up will fall in one of those four categories.

You probably have heard about the importance of creating SMART goals. If not, here is a quick review. SMART is an acronym that stands for Specific, Measurable, Action-oriented, Realistic, and

Time-bound.

Specific. Your goals shouldn't be vague or general. The clearer and more specific you can be in writing your goals the better.

Measurable. If you cannot measure how close you are to accomplishing your goal, it is not an effective goal. You should always know where the finish line is and how far away you are. When you complete your goal, you should be able to check it off on your list.

Action-Oriented. Goals should be things you do, not things you think about, plan or feel. They are things that you actively engage in, not passively wait for.

Realistic. Don't set goals that you cannot achieve. That will only lead to discouragement and quitting. They need to be realistic goals or else you'll give up.

Time-Bound. Goals need a deadline on the calendar. And someday is not a day on the calendar.

This is your assignment. For each of your job descriptions, write out your goals for that area. Make sure they are SMART goals.

Here are some examples of my goals:

[Life Account #1 – Christian]

SMART Goals:
- *I will develop a consistent morning habit of personal devotions that I stick with.*
- *People, especially my wife, will notice that I am less angry and impatient and more of joyful.*

[Life Account #2 – Husband]

SMART Goals:
- *My wife feels more cared for.*
- *We go on regular dates.*
- *We have developed an intentional rhythm where we talk and pray on a regular basis.*

[Life Account #3 – Health]

SMART Goals:
- *I have more energy.*
- *I weigh 180 lbs.*
- *I sleep better at night, and I'm less grumpy with the kids.*

Those are examples of my SMART Goals that I created for myself. I believe that if I am intentional, I can achieve these goals and that would help me reach my vision. It's your turn to write out your goals for your life accounts.

CHAPTER 7

F is for Focus

✳ ✳ ✳

Finding Our Focus

What is most important? What is essential? What is necessary? What is the priority of your life? Those questions are harder to answer than it seems.

We think we know what's important but we don't. We think we have all our priorities straight, but the fact that we have so many priorities shows that we don't really understand what a priority is. Priority comes from the word for one or first. There should only be one priority, not three or five. Not first level and second level. Just one.

The former CEO of Chrysler, Lee Iacocca, was asked what was the secret of his success. He replied,

"The main thing is to keep the main thing the main thing." Even though he created the terrible cars like the Ford Pinto and the Chrysler LaBaron, that's great advice. Find what's important, make it the priority, and focus on it. Simple genius.

Mary and Martha

This reminds me of the story of when Jesus pops in to visit Mary and Martha unannounced. I don't like it when people just stop by the crib without letting me know first. Actually, I don't even like it when people call me without texting me first to let me know that they're about to call. It's rude and intrusive.

I could be busy or preoccupied. I could be on an awesome streak just killin' it on *Candy Crush*. Or I could be having a bad day. The Lakers could have just lost a game or the Clippers could have won one. I could be arguing with my wife or yelling at my kids. It might not be a good idea for you to pop on over without warning. Just saying.

But that's what Jesus does to Mary and Martha. Martha is obviously the first-born in birth order, and Mary the youngest. I should know. I'm the youngest in my family and I'm married to a first-born. They are happy to see Jesus but they show it in very different ways. Mary sits with Jesus and visits with him. We know that Jesus is masterful story-teller. He can captivate a room as well as any Irishman at a pub or a Cajun at a crawfish boil.

I imagine Mary listening to Jesus recall stories of their latest adventures, punctuating the punchline with an uncontrollable snorting laughter like my wife does. The sound of her own snort embarrasses her. This makes her laugh even more uncontrollably, leading to still more snorting, resulting in a chain-reaction of gut-hurting, belly-toning laughter spreading to the disciples. Like the pie-eating contest in *Stand by Me*, it was a complete and total *snort-a-rama*.

Everyone is laughing and enjoying themselves, even Judas chuckles a bit. Everyone except Martha. When Martha hears her sister laugh and snort, she is not amused. She is annoyed. Her frustration grows and her blood begins to boil. When she saw Jesus at her door, she wanted to honor Him and express her gratitude by making Him something to eat. Martha's language of love was spoken in the first century equivalent of casseroles.

Now cooking a meal back then wasn't easy nor spontaneous. You couldn't pull something out of the freezer and open cans of cream of mushroom and whip up a tasty casserole to satisfy the crowd. Even if they did have Campbell's Soup back then, the can opener hadn't even been invented yet. And there were no refrigerators or ovens. If you wanted to cook something, you had to gather wood and build a fire.

Making a meal for the Lord Jesus Christ was no easy task because He never traveled alone. He always had a posse of at least twelve disciples with Him. Imagine trying to feed thirteen dudes that showed up at your door unannounced. If that happened to me today, there's a 50/50 chance that I wouldn't even answer the door. If I were to see you roll up like that in my driveway, I would probably pretend I'm not home like I do on Halloween when the neighbor kids come trick-or-treating.

Thirteen unexpected people over for dinner is a lot to prepare for. That's an entire basketball team plus the coach. How do you feed that many people? Martha doesn't have a deep freezer. There's no Costco nearby. She's got to go and kill some chickens or a goat or something! She has to slaughter an animal and skin it or pluck chicken feathers. That's a lot of work.

So, it's completely understandable that Martha gets frustrated and begins to passive-aggressively chide her sister by asking Jesus, "Can you tell Miss Snorty McLazy I need her help in the kitchen?"

Bless her heart. Martha means well. I love to cook for friends. That's how I show my love. I express my love through tender slow smoked pork products seasoned with my homemade BBQ rub. When you see that beautiful pink smoke ring on my ribs, you know you are loved. I understand Martha's stress. She's worried that she's not doing enough to express her love and gratitude to Jesus. She wants Him to feel welcomed and honored in her home.

Jesus answered her, "Martha, Martha, you are anxious and worried about many things, but only one thing is necessary."

Jesus wanted her to know that not everything is of equal importance. Some things are more important than others. Sure, being hospitable is good, but that's not what is most important to Jesus at that moment. The priority wasn't serving Jesus, it was sitting with Jesus. That was the thing that Jesus cared most about. He didn't come over to get something to eat. He came over to visit with His dear friends.

In Martha's attempt to serve Jesus, she missed what was the most important thing – to sit with Jesus and enjoy His presence.

That's what my wife keeps telling me on date night.

I ask her, "So what do you want to do tonight?"

She answers, "Oh, nothing. I just want to spend time with you."

"Spend time doing what? Do you want to see a movie? Go shopping? What do you want to do? I don't get it."

"Whatever."

The Bible doesn't describe how the Mary and Martha story ends. I like to think that Martha got the message and took off her apron and sat down with Jesus and enjoyed His company for the rest of the day.

There's a lesson for us here. The lesson is that we can't do everything. And everything is not of equal importance. We must choose. We can't sit with Jesus and cook dinner for Jesus at the same time. Choosing to sit with Jesus meant they weren't eating a home-cooked supper that day. (Well, unless Jesus could do something with those leftover fish and loaves.)

There can only be one thing that is most important in any situation. We need to discover what is a priority and what is not. Once we have that clear in our minds, the next step is to discipline ourselves to focus on that priority.

Focusing on what's most important is harder than it sounds. For you to do this, you must ignore everything else. I imagine that it was extremely difficult for Martha to stop cooking and visit with Jesus.

Curly's One Thing

One of my favorite movies is *City Slickers* with Billy Crystal and Jack Palance. Palance won an Oscar for his portrayal of the grisly old cowboy/sage named Curly.

Curly asks Mitch (Billy Crystal's character), "Do you know what the secret of life is?"

Mitch answers, "No. What?"

Curly holds up one finger and says, "This."

"Your finger?"

"One thing. Just one thing." Curly says. "You stick to that and everything else don't mean _____ (insert suitable Christian replacement for a 4-letter word for fecal matter here)."

"That's great," says Mitch. "But what's the one thing?"

"That's what you've got to figure out," Curly replies with a satisfied smile.

The screenwriters got this one right. Focus on what's important and everything else will fall into place. Inspired by this scene, Gary Keller wrote an amazing book called *The One Thing*. Keller is the founder of Keller Williams, which is the largest real estate company in the nation. I highly recommend this book. It's my favorite business and leadership book, second to only *Good to Great* by Jim Collins.

Keller says that the reason most people don't reach their potential or accomplish their goals is because they allow the trivial many things in life crowd out the vital few. We must realize that having five top priorities really means nothing is a priority. Because if everything is equally important, nothing really is. We need to stop juggling, spinning plates, tending multiple irons in the fire, or whatever other metaphor there is for multitasking.

Multitasking doesn't work, or at least it doesn't work well. It's not an efficient or an effective way to get stuff done. Trying to do too many things at the same time doesn't lead to a life of productivity. It leads to stress and mediocrity.

Peripheral Opponents

This leads us to the discipline of focus. *Focus* is the third core component of the *LIFE Path*. Once we have our destination set by our *Legacy* statements and we've worked out our job descriptions and goals with *Intentionality*, then we can move to the disciplined *Focus* stage. We need to focus on what really matters in life.

It takes a lot of discipline to ignore what former Lakers Coach Pat Riley called *peripheral opponents*. In the 80s during the Show-Time era, Riley had a tough time keeping his team focused on winning because of the demands, allure, and temptations of the lifestyles of the rich and famous. He told future Hall of Famers Magic, Kareem, and Worthy that everything off the practice court was a peripheral opponent.

Their true opponents were not even their rival the Boston Celtics. Their only true opponents were themselves. They were their own biggest obstacle and the greatest threat to sports immortality. Pat Riley believed that if they ignored everything else, and just focused on working hard in practice that nothing could stop them from creating a basketball dynasty. *Focus* was the key to their success.

Our problem is we spend too much time and effort in battle with our own peripheral opponents. When you face a peripheral opponent, even if you win that match, you don't accomplish anything because it wasn't your main priority. The secret is knowing what is truly important in your life. This is your primary opponent or goal. And it takes discipline to ignore the peripheral and focus on the primary.

The Success List

If you are like most people I know, you have a long To Do List. You write all the things that you need to get done every day and try to work your way down the list. I personally love To Do Lists. I love checking off the boxes because it makes me feel productive. Sometimes I even write down a task that I have already completed just so I can feel the satisfaction of checking the box. But the To Do List fools us into believing that everything on the list is equally important. My list includes things that must get done like filing my tax return, and things of lesser importance like getting a new movie from RedBox. If I evaluate my To Do List objectively, there may be only one or two things on there that are truly vital.

Here's a suggestion. Instead of having a To Do List, it would be better to create a To Don't List or a Stop Doing List. Or do what Gary Keller suggests and instead of creating a lengthy list of everything you should get done, you should create a *Success List*. I love this idea. It's brilliant.

A *Success List* is a list of the most important activities that you should focus on. Over time, if you focus on doing the activities and behaviors you put on your *Success List*, they will lead you to accomplish your intentional goals.

The key to success is doing the basics well most of the time. It is focusing on the fundamentals until you master them. The secret to productivity and success is to find out what really matters and focus on that by ignoring everything else.

For example, a basketball player's *Success List* will include practicing jump shots, ball-handling drills, and conditioning. A parent's *Success List* will include quality time, meals together, and words of affirmation. A salesperson's *Success List* includes prospecting, networking, and presentations. The *Success List* for Christian spiritual growth involves Bible study, prayer, and commitment to the Body of Christ.

The Focusing Question

So how do we find our *Success List*? Here's one question to ask that will help you discover what you need to focus on. I call it the *Focusing Question*.

> *What two or three on-going behaviors, that over time with consistent and focused effort, would lead me to accomplish this goal?*

This is a strategic question. Let me explain how this question works.

1) It identifies specific behaviors.
We are trying to find useful and impactful behavior to focus on and commit to. We are not interested in ideas or emotions. We are looking for things we need to do. We are looking for actions, not ideas. We'll talk about the power of building habits in the next chapter.

2) These behaviors should be on-going and consistent.
This behavior needs to be something that we can do repeatedly. It is of little use to write down something that you cannot commit to. These behaviors should be small things that you can do consistently and integrate into your lifestyle. Too many people make high commitments that they cannot keep. We are looking for a lifestyle change, not a failed New Year's resolution.

3) These behaviors should be "lead measures."
The team at Franklin Covey wrote a book called *The Four Disciplines of Execution* that explain the helpful

difference between Lead Measures and Lag Measures. The SMART goals that we set earlier are Lag Measures. A Lag Measure is the measurement of a goal you are trying to accomplish. It's called a Lag because by the time you get the data the result has already happened.

Lag Measures measure the goal you are trying to accomplish. Lag Measures are important but once you see a Lag Measure, there's nothing you can do about it because it's in the past. For example, if you have a goal of losing weight by your wedding day when that day comes there's nothing you can do to improve it because it already happened. You can try to lose weight in the future, but nothing can be done about your wedding day.

Lead Measures are different because they are predictive and influenceable. Being predictive means that you believe that if you do this behavior, then you can predict you will have good results. And being influenceable means that you can tweak it and change it along the way.

4) There should be only two or three behaviors.

You can only choose two or three behaviors. You can't have more than that or it will be too hard to keep track of. Apply the 80/20 Rule (or the Pareto Principle). You get 80% of your results from only 20% of your activities. Certain activities just have greater value and leverage. Find out which behaviors help you achieve the results you want.

Let me give you some examples of how all this works together. I'll show you how I personally applied the *Focusing Question* in my life to discover my *Success List*.

For example, here's my purpose and vision for my personal relationship with Jesus:

> *I am a follower of Jesus. My purpose is to pursue a growing relationship with Jesus exhibited by increasing intimacy, trust, joy, and gratitude. I am passionately pursuing a closer relationship Him. I am growing to love, trust, and enjoy Him more every day. I am full of gratitude and joy because of my growing relationship with Him.*

That's my goal for my relationship with God. I know it's not edited well and there's lots of repetition. (I wrote that on a meaningful and tearful day on the beach so I decided to keep it as is because it still speaks to me.)

Now let me apply the *Focusing Question* to this

area of my life.

What two or three on-going behaviors, that over time with consistent and focused effort, would lead me to accomplish this goal?

I could write down lots of things that could help me. I could write down listening to praise and worship music, sermons on podcast, reading good books, going to conferences, etc. There are lots of things that I can do. But I only chose three things to focus on.

Here's my Success List for my personal spiritual growth:

1) Daily Devotions
2) Writing in my journal every day
3) Weekly personal retreat of at least 4 hours

That's it. That's all I focus on for my personal spiritual growth. Notice I don't have anything about prayer meetings, fasting, or even Bible Study. I just put down the basics. I have learned that if I focus on doing those three behaviors, my faith grows and expands to the other spiritual disciplines as well. But if I ignore one of those basics, the other areas begin to run dry too.

I want you to find which behaviors will lead you to accomplish your goal. Then once you know what they are, focus on those behaviors. This is your *Success List*. Ignore everything else. Do the basics well most of the time, and you will be successful in reaching your goals.

Let's look at another area of my life - my personal health and fitness.

Goal and Vision for Personal Health:

I am in the best shape of my adult life. I have more than enough energy to keep up with the stresses and demands of life without getting tired or grumpy. I weigh 180 lbs. and live an active life with my children. We enjoy doing active things together as a family such as jogging, biking, and hiking.

This is a huge area of weakness. I like food. I don't just like to eat food, I actually think about food. I'm thinking about what I'm going to eat for lunch right now while I'm writing this sentence. I'm overweight and I hate working out. I used to play basketball but several injuries make it too painful for me now. My job as a pastor and writer doesn't help. I mostly sit at a desk all day. For reference, here's what I wrote as my *Current Reality* a few months ago when I last updated my *LIFE Path*.

Health - Current Reality
- I weigh 208 lbs
- I don't sleep well
- I have serious acid reflux issues
- I get tired and grumpy and lose my patience with my family too often
- My left knee and both ankles hurt. I can't play basketball or run without hurting. My cardio is terrible.

Let's apply the *Focusing Question* to this area of my personal health.

What two or three on-going behaviors, that over time with consistent and focused effort, would lead me to accomplish this goal?

Here's my *Success List* for my health account.
1) Track what I eat.
2) No more sugar in coffee and soda.
3) Ten sets of "office workouts" daily.

That's it. I don't have anything about going on a diet, joining a gym, or doing P90X on my list. That's because I tried all those things and I don't stick with them for long. I know myself. I won't do anything that is too hard, so I needed to make minor changes in my behavior that I can stick to. But since I started tracking my meals, it's encouraged me to stop eating fast food and pack a lunch from home. I use Splenda in my coffee and drink Diet Dr. Pepper now. And I do little exercises around the office throughout the day.

It doesn't seem like much but it all adds up over time. When I created this goal a few months ago, I weighed 208 lbs. Since then I lost ten pounds without even trying much. I also sleep a lot better now. By focusing on these small on-going behaviors, I'm starting to make some progress. I'm not giving anyone health advice. *Mr. Kettle, meet Mr. Pot.* I'm just trying to do the basics well and it's beginning to show fruit.

Goals are for Losers

Take your time and answer the *Focusing Question* for each area of your life. Once you have created your *Success List* of behaviors that will lead you to accomplish each of your goals, I'm going to ask you to do something that will seem illogical.

Once you have your *Success List*, I want you to

forget about your goals. Ignore them. Put them away and don't look at them. At least for a while. Just focus on practicing your *Success List*.

Your *Success List* is like getting in the gym and putting in practice. "You talkin' bout practice!?" asked Allen Iverson. Yeah, I'm talkin' bout practice!

If you are a pro basketball player with the goal of winning the NBA Championship, how would you go about accomplishing that goal? It doesn't matter how good you are, winning the championship is not something that you can control by yourself. You cannot control if someone on your team gets injured, or if your rival makes a blockbuster trade to improve their team. You cannot control the biased whistles of the nearsighted zebras or lucky bounces or technical fouls. Just ask Draymond Green.

The only thing you can control is what you do during practice. You may not be able to control what the other team is going to do, but you can control how many jumpers you put up in practice each day. You can control your conditioning and improve your ball handling. Practice time is where you learn to integrate the *Success List*. Over time, if you get your butt into the gym each morning, run sprints, put up a thousand jumpers, and work on your ball-handling, you will greatly improve your chances of making that game-winning play in Game 7 of the NBA Finals.

But while you're in the gym, you cannot think about Game 7. The only thing you should focus on is the work that you got to put in that day. You got to focus on the basics because doing the basics well most of the time will lead to success.

Years ago, I joined Weight Watchers because I wanted to lose weight. I didn't stick with it too long because I was usually the only guy in a room full of pudgy women in stretch pants. That's not the real reason I quit. I quit because of the stupid weigh in. They weighed you at the beginning of every meeting and recorded it in your little book. I was trying to eat right by counting my food points, but I wasn't seeing the results on the scale I thought I should be seeing. I got discouraged and I quit.

Former NFL running back, Reggie Rivers said in his TED Talk that "if you want to achieve your goals, don't focus on them. Focus on your behavior." Sometimes the progress we are making is so small that it is unnoticeable and impossible to measure. If the only feedback is the scale or another milestone, it's easy to become discouraged.

Scott Adams, the creator of the Dilbert comics, wrote a helpful and hilarious book on productivity called *How to Fail at Almost Everything and Still Win*

Big. In it, he has a chapter called *Goals are for Losers*. He says that focusing on your goals gives you a loser's mentality. This is because every day you don't accomplish your goal, you're a loser. You're only a winner on the one day you reach your goal and a loser on every other day.

He suggests focusing on your daily commitments instead. This will encourage you and give you a winner's mentality. Because you are a winner if you accomplish those two or three things on your *Success List*. This builds momentum and empowers you with encouragement.

I advise you not to focus on the Weight Watchers scale of your goals. Set your goals. Use them to create your *Success List* and then ignore your goals. Just focus on your behaviors. Focus on doing those two or three things on your *Success List* every day. If you are consistent, over time you will see results. I don't ignore my goals forever. I usually check them once or twice a quarter to evaluate if my *Success List* is producing any results. If it doesn't, I may consider tweaking them a little.

CHAPTER 8

E is for Execution

***

The Sword and the Trowel

Charles Spurgeon published a newsletter called *The Sword and the Trowel* for pastors and Christian leaders. These newsletters have been compiled into volumes that contain ministry lessons, life wisdom, and inspiration to many.

Spurgeon took the name of his publication from the story of Nehemiah. In Nehemiah 4, we see the Israelites beginning to make progress on rebuilding the wall of Jerusalem. Then the mockers and critics come out of the woodwork. They're like internet trolls that throw shade and snarky criticism about the work.

The head troll was a windbag named Sanballat. The Bible said that when he heard about this project, "he was angry and greatly enraged and he jeered at the Jews" (Nehemiah 4:1).

He does a total punk move and takes his crew to mock and make fun of the hardworking Israelites. He's like that pock-marked, crater-faced leader of the Scorpions in the movie *Grease* that makes fun of Kenickie's car.

When Craterface runs into his car Kenickie shouts, "Hey, that's my car you hit!"

Crater Face replies, "That piece of junk? I'll pay you 75 cents for that thing... and your chick!"

Sanballet's crew start throwing serious shade at Nehemiah's T-Birds:

What are these feeble Jews doing?

Why are you working so hard? You think you're going to finish it in a day?

Will they revive the stones out of the heaps of rubbish and burned ones at that?

A little fox can break down their stone wall!

Sanballat laughs as he races off in his pimped-out 1949 Mercury with flames coming out of the tailpipes. Nehemiah does everything he can to ignore those peripheral opponents. He knows his real opponent is that wall. The work itself. If he gives in and engages his critics, they win because they succeeded in distracting him from the work. Nehemiah and the Israelites endure and continue to focus on the work. The Bible says, "the people had a mind to work" (Neh. 4:6). They were dialed in and focused.

The Scorpions ramp it up and now they mean business. Now they want to race for pinks. Pinks?

"Pinks, you punk! Pink slips? Ownership papers!"

"And the rules are there ain't no rules."

This is where the gloves come off and Sanballat starts to plot, threaten, and conspire. This is no longer a time for words and insults. Things escalate quickly to aggressive action, a show of force, and impending violence. Sanballat gathers his crew for a surprise attack on the Israelites. He was hoping to catch the workers off guard and kill a few of them to discourage the other workers and stop the work.

But Nehemiah was prepared for this. He told his

men to be ready to work and to fight. The Bible describes how the Israelites went to work, "each labored on the work with one hand and held his weapon with the other. And each of the builders had his sword strapped at his side while he built" (Neh. 4:17-18).

This is where Spurgeon the idea for *The Sword and the Trowel*. A trowel is a tool that masons use to slap concrete on bricks when building a wall. Symbolically, the sword represents the Word of God or holy work. The trowel represents the menial labor of secular and ordinary life. Every Christian needs to have both tools and know how to use them well.

Churches and pastors focus on helping Christians learn how to wield the sword well - to pray, to know the Bible, to serve God, etc. But we're not so good at teaching people how to use the trowel. The problem is that most of life is not done with sword work, but trowel work.

Most churches do well at teaching their people theology and the spiritual dynamics of life but are not so good at teaching practical and necessary lessons of goal setting, productivity, self-leadership, building habits, and organization. I think this has to do with our hesitation to learn from non-Christian sources. For some reason, a lot of Christians don't think they can learn anything from people outside the Church. I think this is arrogant. I've read and benefited from the wisdom of leaders, creatives, and thinkers from many fields. Doesn't the Word say in I Thessalonians 5:21, "Prove all things; hold fast that which is good"? I'm going to share with you some of the best lessons I've learned.

I want to help you learn how to use both the sword and the trowel well. In this chapter, we will discuss the final component of the *LIFE Path*. The "E" stands for *execution*. I want to show you how to tie everything together into a tangible *LIFE Path* and show you how to implement that plan.

But before we go any further, let's do a little review to make sure we're on the same page. If you've been following along, you should have created a *Legacy* document that includes how you want people to remember you and the eulogy that you hope would be read at your funeral. You also should have an *Intentional* plan that involves job descriptions with SMART goals for the different areas of your life. Then you should have a *Success List* with 2-3 behaviors that you will *Focus* on that will help you accomplish your goals.

Great. Now, in this chapter, I want to get as practical as I can. I want to talk to you about your commitment, behaviors, and habits. I'll give you some of my best productivity tips and tricks that have helped me along the way.

Execution is about following the game plan. Usually, this is where plans fall apart. Plans and goals look beautiful on a piece of paper pinned to our wall. But if what is written on the wall isn't happening down the hall, that piece of paper is useless. Most plans don't become reality due to poor implementation. Again, as Mike Tyson said, "Everybody has a plan until they get punched in the face."

We need to make sure our *LIFE Path* can get punched in the face by reality and still survive. The following are some valuable concepts that have helped me successfully execute my *LIFE Path*.

The Compound Effect

Darren Hardy, the author of *The Compound Effect* says that smart choices consistently applied will lead to remarkable results. He calls this the compound effect and we see it at work in Nehemiah's story. It was Nehemiah's dedicated consistency of stacking one stone on top of another without stopping for 52 days that finished the wall.

The compound effect says that consistency over

time is much more valuable than infrequent moments of inspiration and intensity. You may have heard about the illustration of the compound effect called the *magic penny*, but I'll remind you of it again.

Imagine a rich person wanted to give you and me a bunch of money, and he gave us the choice of how we would receive this money.

Option 1 - Take $3 million today.

Option 2 - Take a penny today, and he will double what you have every day for 31 days straight.

Which option would you choose?

You choose Option 1 that will give you $3 million cash money today and you take your family to Sizzler's.

I choose Option 2, which is the magic penny option. So, on Day 1, I only have one cent. That penny doubles on Day 2, and I now have two cents. It doubles again on Day 3, and now I have four cents. I'm starting to get worried that I made the wrong choice. But I endure.

On Day 10, I only have $5.12. Shoot! I'm a third of the way through the month and I can't even super-size my Big Mac meal. One Day 15, my stash grows to $163.84. I'm half of the way through and nowhere near what you got. But this is where the compound effect starts to pick up momentum. On Day 20, I have $5,242.88. Only eleven days left. What's going to happen?

Miraculously, on Day 30, my magic penny grows to $5.4 million! I have surpassed your $3 million but looky here: I got one more day left. Yee Ha!

By Day 31, my magic penny has grown to over $10.7 million. Over three times more than you got. Now I'm going buy my own Sizzler's franchise!

That's the power of the compound effect at work. You just keep adding one rock to that wall at a time and before you know it, you've done what everyone thought was impossible.

It's all about consistency and commitment. Five minutes in the Word each day and you can get through at least half the Bible in a year. Cutting out sugar and doing a few push-ups everyday has helped me lose weight and become more active. One word of affirmation each day over 30 years will lead to a beautiful marriage.

Again, we should listen to the advice of my mentor Bill Wellons: *Start Small. Go Deep. Dream Big.*

Gateway Behaviors

One of Isaac Newton's *Laws of Motion* can be very useful to help us make progress on our *LIFE Path*. His first law of motion is referred to as Law of Inertia and Momentum which states:

An object at rest tends to stay at rest.

An object in motion tends to stay in motion.

According to Newton's first law, the most difficult thing is moving from a state of rest to a state of motion. Or in laymen's terms, the hardest part is just starting. Once you begin, you break the force of inertia, and you have momentum working on your side.

They say that a space shuttle uses up most its fuel getting off the launch pad. After it builds enough momentum to break through earth's gravity, everything becomes easier.

Jim Collins calls this the *flywheel effect*. The hardest thing about working out is getting your butt off the couch and into the car. Once you're in the gym, it's not so hard. The hardest thing about doing your devotions is waking up early and opening your Bible. Once you do that, it's easy-peasy-lemon-squeezy.

My bed has an incredibly strong force of gravity, especially in the mornings. I can hardly get up. And in the afternoon, that force of gravity is somehow transferred to my couch. They have tractor-beams that pull me in. But once I break their grip, I have enough momentum to go about my day and work on my *Success List*.

So, the secret is figuring out ways to just get started. This is what world-renowned ballerina and choreographer Twyla Tharp talks about in her book, *The Creative Habit*. She religiously works out two hours each morning even though she is now in her 60s. She says that it has become increasingly more difficult to motivate her old bones to wake up early and go the studio each day to work out. Thinking about a two-hour workout can be overwhelming when you're lying in bed debating if you should skip the workout for the day.

So, she makes a small commitment to herself. She doesn't have to work out two hours each day. All she has to do is put on her dance clothes and get into a cab. Not work out. But just get dressed and get into a cab. Once she is in the cab, she could change her mind and get out of the cab and go upstairs and get back into bed without guilt because she has already kept the commitment she has made to herself.

But she never does. Once in the cab, she has already broken the gravitational pull of inertial and has begun to build of up momentum for the day.

She thinks, "Heck, I'm already dressed and in the

cab. I might as well go to the gym."

Let's apply this idea. You need to think of small micro behaviors that are so easy to accomplish that you can do it even on your worst day. I've heard of an author who never experiences writer's block because he commits to writing at least fifty words each morning whether he feels like it or not.

I call these *gateway behaviors*. Just think "gateway drug" but put a positive spin on it. A *gateway behavior* is a small action that you take that will lead to other, bigger actions. If you have a messy home, a *gateway behavior* could be committing to clean up for one minute when you get home before you turn on the TV. Or washing two dishes before bedtime. Once you get started, you've broken the power of inertia and you've got momentum on your side.

This is opposite from what success guru Brian Tracy recommends in his book *Eat That Frog*. He says that you should do the most demanding and difficult thing first. If you get it out of the way first, the rest your day becomes easier. But if I tried to follow that advice, I would never get out of bed or I would procrastinate all day. I find it easier to start small with these *gateway behaviors* because it allows me to build up momentum. I start to feel good about myself and I have more energy to tackle the bigger things later.

I've applied this principle in my personal devotions and I've made a huge breakthrough in this area. I read a lot, but I've never had a consistent Quiet Time for personal devotions. I employed the *gateway behavior* concept to my personal devotional time with God. I committed to reading at least one verse and writing out one prayer each day. I can do this in about seventeen seconds. But once I get my Bible and journal out and I start reading, it's almost impossible to stop at just one verse and one prayer.

On most days, I now read several chapters of the Bible and write an average of three pages in my prayer journal. This *gateway behavior* of one verse and one prayer has revolutionized my relationship with God. Even on the days I don't feel well or am running late, I still have time for my one verse and one prayer. I don't feel guilty if that's all I do on those days because I still fulfilled my commitment.

Look through your goals and *Success List*. How can you apply the *gateway behavior* concept in your life?

The Power of Habit

What is a habit? A habit is a learned behavior that you do almost involuntarily. It takes no effort at all to do because it is just a part of your life. I don't have to remind myself to brush my teeth because I've been doing it all my life. Once a habit is set, it takes no work to keep it up.

Our goal is to intentionally take the behaviors on your *Success List* and turn them into life-long habits. Once you do that, everything becomes easier.

Charles Duhigg says habits have three parts. Habits are made up of a cycle of a *trigger* that leads to a *routine* because of an anticipated *reward*. *Trigger*, then *routine*, then *reward*. I recommend reading his book *The Power of Habit* if you want to dive in deeper with the science of habit formation.

Habits can be your friend or your enemy. It's hard to create and break habits regardless of if they are good or bad. Therefore, it would be smart to leverage the power of habit to work in your favor.

The problem with most attempts at personal growth or self-improvement is that they are usually dependent on making wise decisions and being self-disciplined. But we are only given a finite quantity of willpower and motivation each day. It takes a lot of energy and motivation to decide to do the things on your *Success List*. It's like what Paul says in Romans 7 about doing what he doesn't want to do and not doing what he does, or something like that. The problem isn't that you don't know what you should be doing. The problem is that at the moment you need to make that decision you don't have enough willpower to choose wisely.

The key is, since our willpower is so fickle and undependable, we should take it out of the equation altogether. How do we do that? Well, we take willpower out of the equation by building good habits. Once you create habits, your behaviors become almost involuntary and require no willpower to get the job done. Does that make sense? It is much easier to try to create a healthy life pattern of behavior. Once your habits are set, these behaviors become involuntary.

Let's talk about your personal devotions for a minute. Whether call it a Quiet Time or Lectio Divina or JAM (Jesus and Me) Session for your soul, you need to develop this into a habit. I can't think of a single growing Christian that is mature and used by God that has not developed this habit in their lives. This habit needs to be so ingrained that you involuntarily reach for the Bible each day. Like brushing your teeth, it feels unnatural if you don't. It needs to be something that you do even on the days you're walking through the valley of the shadow of death. Because I guarantee that if you haven't developed this habit, you won't have the energy or motivation to start when you really need it.

Don't Break the Chain

Jerry Seinfeld is one of the most successful comedians of all time. He was asked what was the secret of his success.

He says, "I write at least one joke a day. Every day."

Seinfeld uses a simple wall calendar to track his commitment. Every day that he writes a joke, he draws a big red "X" on that day. He creates a chain of days and his goal is to never miss a day. The jokes don't even have to be good. And he only has to write one a day. But he attributes the success to his daily consistency of writing at least one new joke a day.

This is how I finished my doctoral dissertation. I was stuck and overwhelmed at the research. I had been working on it for six years and I wanted to quit. I didn't like the subject of my research and I wanted to change the topic of my dissertation. I was so discouraged because I had so much work to do. The mountain seemed too insurmountable. Most days, I didn't even have enough energy or motivation to get started on it.

Then I tried Seinfeld's method. I got a calendar from the dollar store that served no other purpose other than track my dissertation project. I made the commitment to working on my dissertation for 15 minutes a day (*gateway behavior*). If I put in my 15 minutes, I got to draw a big 'X' on that day. It didn't even have to be a productive 15 minutes. But I couldn't skip a day. It wasn't a Nehemiah level accomplishment, but I finished by doctoral dissertation in only a few months after I started using this method.

The key is to track one behavior and not miss a day. This behavior should be a small *gateway behavior* to get you started. Do it consistently. Don't miss a day. If you do miss one day, you must make sure you do not miss two. If you miss a day, your top priority for the next day is to complete your assignment. If you miss two days, you have broken the chain.

When and Where

Jon Acuff says that if you don't write down your goals, you will almost certainly not achieve them. About 35% of people who write it down their goals will accomplish their goals. One out of three isn't bad. But there's one simple hack that you can do that will double the likelihood that you will keep your commitment and accomplish your goal. He says that 70% of people who do this one simple thing accomplish their goals. Do you know what that is?

He calls it your *When & Where*. If you take your goal or your *Success List* and take the additional effort to determine the time and location you will work on that activity, you will double your effectiveness.

The reason this concept is so powerful is that it leverages one of the basic elements of habits. Habits start with a trigger that reminds you to do your routine. In my experience, the most powerful triggers are time and place. When I wake up and go to the bathroom, I instinctive reach for the toothbrush even though I'm not even fully awake. The time and place triggered my routine without any effort on my part. When I get to my office early in the morning, I involuntarily grab my Bible and my journal. The *when & where* became my trigger for my new habit.

When you commit to doing a specific behavior at a specific time and location, the time and place will reinforce and remind you of the behavior that you're supposed to engage in.

For each behavior on your *Success List*, write down a when and a where. If you do this, it will double the likelihood you will keep your commitment. This small step just may change your life.

Create a Scoreboard

I'm a competitive person and I need the scoreboard to keep me motivated. Activities without scoreboards don't keep me engaged. I created a scoreboard for myself of daily or weekly things that I use to track my behavior.

This list of behaviors that I track acts as a dashboard for my life. My scoreboard helps me keep track of the commitments I've made to myself. I pick one behavior from each of my *Success Lists* and track it on my scoreboard. I pick one that is a lead measure or *gateway behavior* to track.

Why do I only track one behavior for each area? Because if I have eight areas, and each has three *Success List* behaviors, then I would have to track 24 behaviors. That's way too much. I only want one thing to track for each area of my life.

Below are the behaviors that I am currently tracking on my personal scoreboard:

1) Out of the house before 7 AM
2) One verse and one prayer
3) Review my eulogy
4) Write 200 words

5) Contact one person from church
6) Write down one thing I appreciate about my wife
7) Plan my day in my Bullet Journal
8) Give one affirmation to each child

That scoreboard is the product and summary of my entire *LIFE Path*. I constantly monitor and adjust what I measure. If the behavior I pick to measure isn't a good *gateway behavior* because it doesn't lead to other behaviors, then I pick something else. I track my scoreboard on my smartphone with an app called *Don't Break the Chain*. This is a paid app, but there are some similar free ones out there.

The wonderful thing about my scoreboard is that it gives me valuable feedback. I can track my progress. It helps me feel successful and encouraged because I know that if I'm intentional in following this path it will eventually get me to the destination of the legacy I desire to have.

Manage Your Energy

I recently got the privilege to meet someone I deeply respect. Carey Nieuwhof is a pastor, author, speaker, blogger, podcaster, butcher, baker, and candlestick maker. He's the ministry equivalent of those Jamaicans from that *In Living Color* skit. "You only got trreee jobs mon? You lazy bum! I got fifffteeen jobs mon!"

I asked Carey how he manages to get everything done. I wanted to learn how he could be so productive and have a family and be a normal guy. I imagined he must be great at managing his time.

What he told me shifted my thinking about how I approach productivity. He says you cannot manage time at all. Time moves forward at a constant rate for everyone.

Instead of managing your time, he says, you need to learn how to manage your energy. He invited me to participate in a new video-based course he created called *The High Impact Leader*. The course teaches you "how to get time, energy, and priorities working in your favor."

I highly recommend taking this ten session course. It's not open all the time and it costs money, but it's a great investment. This course really helped me. You can get more information at **www.careynieuwhof.com**.

I won't give away all of Carey's secrets, but the biggest A-HA lesson was when he said this:

Do your best work when you're at your best.

That's great advice. He recommends tracking your energy level to determine when you're at your best. Some people are night people, others are morning people. Once you figure out when you function best, you need to block out your schedule during those hours to devote to your most important work. If you're a morning person, do not waste your most productive hours by checking email first thing when you get to the office.

Carey suggests creating an ideal week. My friend Brian Howard has some good blog posts on this topic (**www.contextcoaching.com**). An ideal week is a static weekly schedule where you block out chunks of time to devote to certain activities. When you know the times of day you are most creative and productive, that's when you schedule your most important work.

The ideal week has radically improved my personal productivity. I was never a morning person, but I trained myself to become one. Now I love my mornings because this is when I do my writing and work on my sermons. To protect my most productive hours when I have the most energy and focus, I disciplined myself to never check email until lunch time. I have also moved every meeting that I can until after lunch so I can leverage my energy and do my best work when I'm at my best.

The Miracle Morning

As I mentioned earlier, I'm not a natural morning person. I'm a night owl. But I needed to find some extra time to work on my doctoral dissertation. My only available option was to try to wake up early and get some writing in before my regular day started.

I picked up a book called *The Miracle Morning* by Hal Elrod. Wow. This book helped me create a morning routine that has doubled, maybe tripled, my productivity. I can't believe how much more I accomplish now. I can't recommend this book highly enough.

I learned that there's a lot in life that I can't control. I have a church to lead, wife and kids to care for, and many other responsibilities. My calendar is filled up with things I can't control. My wife and I share a Google Calendar account and she puts things on there that I'm supposed to be at. Rehearsals, tutoring, Jiu-Jitsu, small group, dinner with the in-laws, school plays, etc.

There's so much of my day that I can't control. But the one time of the day I have complete control of is my mornings. I understand why Elrod calls it miracle mornings. It has become my sanctuary and bliss. When I have a good morning, it stays with me all day.

Two simple tips that I gleaned from this book helped me a great deal. The first is to move your alarm clock (I use my phone) outside of your bedroom. I plug my phone in and leave it in the kitchen. Each morning when the alarm goes off, I have to get out of bed and go into the kitchen to turn it off. This forces me to get up. He also suggests getting a drink of water because we get dehydrated while we sleep and the water will energize you.

The second helpful tip he gives is to create a morning routine. He uses the acronym SAVERS for his routine. SAVERS stand for Silence, Affirmations, Visualization, Exercise, Reading, and Scribing, but not necessarily in that order.

Inspired by this idea, I created my own morning routine. Can you guess what it is? It's the things on my scoreboard. I do six of the eight things on my scoreboard at the beginning of every morning. This ensures I get the day started on the right foot.

I can't encourage you enough to leverage the power of the becoming an early riser. It has made a dramatic difference in my life.

Do a 30-Day Challenge

You probably feel a bit overwhelmed right now. You have a mountain to climb. You see the path ahead of you clearly but you're a little intimidated because you're not sure you can complete the whole journey. You're not even sure if you want to get started.

Let me give you a little challenge. Just focus on it for 30 days and see what happens. You might be surprised at the result. These 30-day challenges are getting more and more popular. You find people doing 30-day challenges to build habits such as healthy eating, saving money, walking, or gratitude.

After hearing the bestselling author of *Do-Over*, Jon Acuff, speak at a conference about an online course he created called the *30 Days of Hustle*, I decided to take his challenge and join. This was when I was stuck and discouraged in my doctoral work. I needed something to change. I needed a catalyst. Like a personal productivity version of the trainer at the gym.

Jon's *30 Days of Hustle* was the catalyst that I needed to make progress in an area I was stuck in for six years. The 30-day challenge forced me to commit to accomplishing one specific goal and work on it every day for 30 straight days.

During that month, I experienced a huge

breakthrough. It was during those 30 days that I scrapped my former dissertation topic and wrote an entirely new dissertation proposal on a completely new topic I was more passionate about. My new proposal got approved by my doctoral committee and I began research on this project.

After the *30 Days of Hustle* was over, I kept my focus and worked on my dissertation every day. Within six months, I submitted my first draft of my dissertation to my doctoral committee and they accepted my first draft as ready for defense. This is unheard of. Usually, there are second and third drafts and rewrites. But my committee thought my research and writing was good. The 30-day challenge was a catalyst that helped me focus.

Jon's course really helped me experience a huge breakthrough in productivity. You can find out more about the *30 Days of Hustle* on Jon's blog (**www.acuff.me**). But you don't have to take Jon's course to benefit from the lessons I learned. You can come up with your own 30-day challenge.

My breakthrough came when I made the commitment to give my total focus to work on one thing for a predetermined amount of time, 30 days. After those 30 days, I could go back to doing whatever I was doing before, but something happened. Focusing for those 30 days helped me overcome the gravitational pull of inertia and I began to develop the good habits. Then my productivity took off.

Consider giving yourself your own 30-day challenge. For the next 30 days, focus on one thing. Work the system. Follow the steps to creating your *LIFE Path*.

Summary

Execution is about implementing your plan. It's about taking intentional steps and making specific commitments. It is about taking responsibility for yourself and creating good habits.

There are lots of tools and tips out there that you can use. But *execution* really is about determination and commitment. But you have to bring those things to the table. So, let's talk about your next steps.

CHAPTER 9

Next Steps

* * *

Walking on Water

It was a dark and stormy night... (I've always wanted to write that.)

The twelve disciples are in a little boat in a big sea. They're exhausted from a long day of ministry. They're still scratching their heads about how Jesus multiplied the loaves and fishes and fed that huge crowd. It was somehow so miraculous and spectacular and normal and ordinary all at the same time. Just another day with Jesus.

Now they're in this boat in the middle of the night in the worst storm they've ever experienced.

They're in this life-threatening predicament because they obeyed Jesus' instruction to sail to the other side of the Sea of Galilee while He stayed on the shore.

The disciples are all worried and fearful of the storm. The one disciple who is most afraid is Peter. He grew up on the Sea of Galilee. He comes from a long line of fishermen. He knows this storm is bad. Really bad. They're all going to die.

As they madly try to bail water out of the little boat, someone screams.

"A ghost!"

They spot the figure of a man walking towards them on top of the waves.

"It's the Lord!" another shouts when he recognizes Jesus.

Peter smiles. The presence of Jesus gives him comfort. Looking into the face of Jesus, he no longer notices the storm that threatens his life.

"Lord, if you are willing, let me come to you on the water," Peter says.

"Come."

Without thinking Peter steps over the side of the boat and starts walking to Jesus ON THE WATER! He is walking on top of the water?! He is literally a walking miracle. He is defying the very laws of nature. Everyone's jaw drops in amazement.

Then doubt seeps into Peter's mind.

"What am I doing? Am I nuts? I going to drown."

He looks back at the boat and sees how far he has already come. It's too far away to jump back in. He sees that Jesus is still a little way away. Then he notices the wind and the waves. Peter takes his focus off Jesus and starts to think, "How am I going to get myself out of this one?"

Panic begins to set in and he starts to sink. Glug, glug, glug.

Then Peter prays a prayer I've prayed many times.

"Jesus, help me!"

Before Peter reaches the pineapple under the sea, Jesus rescues him and helps him back into the boat.

Jesus smiles and says, "O you of little faith. Why did you doubt?"

We look at Peter's story and we usually point out his failure and near demise. He got scared and nearly drowned. "That sure taught him a lesson right there," we think to ourselves. The lesson being, don't get out of the boat in a storm. Or don't try to start something you can't finish or something like that.

No, the real lesson is *if you want to walk on water you have to get out of the boat.* John Ortberg wrote a book with that title that I didn't read. Just reading the title was so much more than enough to edify my soul that I didn't have to buy the book. (This is how I feel about Eugene Peterson's *The Long Obedience in the Same Direction*, which is another book with a great soul-edifying title that I didn't read.)

Yes, Peter almost drowned. But he was not a failure or a coward that day. There were eleven other disciples who didn't even think about getting out of the boat. Peter is the only person other than Jesus to experience walking on water (even though it was only for a short distance).

Overcoming Fear

I want to be more like Peter. I've played it safe too many times in life. I've stayed in a leaky boat, bailing water to try to keep it from sinking. Sometimes playing it safe is the worst decision you can make.

Personally, I get angry when I think of all the times I doubted God and listened to my fears and insecurities. I shrank back. I didn't take the opportunities that God presented to me. My biggest regret is not believing that God would come through on the promises He made to me. For some reason, I kept questioning, "What if God doesn't come through?"

What is stopping us from stepping out of the boat? The answer is simple. It's fear. We're afraid of so many things. Looking dumb. Taking risks. Failure. Pain. Change. The opinions of others.

We need to learn how to overcome fear. Because everything worthwhile in life that you enjoy today came because you didn't allow fear to stop you. You didn't allow fear to stop you from learning how to ride a bike or swim. Fear didn't stop you from learning to drive or going out on your first date. You wouldn't enjoy any of those things if you allowed fear to stop you. Don't let fear stop you from pursuing your *LIFE Path*.

When we are afraid, we begin to ask the "what if" questions. What if I fail? What if God lets me down? What if I succeed? What if my life changes? What if I'm not ready? What if they laugh at me?

One of the biggest fears we have is that our dreams are too big for God to fulfill. We don't want to be disappointed. We think it's too much to ask for the desires of our heart. But that's not our real problem. Our problem is not that our dreams are too big. It's that our God is too small.

C.S. Lewis preached a sermon called *The Weight of Glory* that includes these brilliant lines:

It would seem that Our Lord finds our desires not too strong, but too weak. We are half-hearted creatures, fooling about with drink and sex and ambition when infinite joy is offered us, like an ignorant child who wants to go on making mud pies in a slum because he cannot imagine what is meant by the offer of a holiday at the sea. We are far too easily pleased.

Yes, we are far too easily pleased. You should know that God wants more for you than what you are currently experiencing. The Gospel demands it.

Romans 8:32 says, "He who did not spare His own Son but gave Him up for us all, how will He not also with Him graciously give us all things?"

Paul is making an argument about the expectation of blessing based on his understanding of the Gospel. His logic is solid. He argues that if God has already shown us that He is incomprehensibly generous and gracious by giving us Jesus as our substitute on the Cross, it would be unthinkable to start thinking of Him as a miserly, stingy God that would withhold blessings from us now.

God wants so much more for you. He wants you to walk with Him on the water over the storms of life. You don't know what amazing things God has in store for you.

I sincerely want you to experience the abundant life that He came to give us. I want you to be like the tree planted be streams of water who yields fruit during harvest and whose leaves are green even in winter. I want my life to be like the Negev after the rain brings streams into the desert and the landscape explodes with wildflowers. The question is, do you?

Next Steps

So, what's next? Great question. Let me suggest some next steps that you can take.

1) Pray for Dissatisfaction

Dissatisfaction is the beginning of change. It's one of the prerequisites that we discussed earlier. Before you can change you need to be sick and tired of being sick and tired. You need to pray that God would plant a seed of heaven in your heart so that you will begin to desire more than the earth can give you.

Paul expressed his greatest desire this way: he said, "I want to know Christ and the power of His resurrection" (Phil. 3:10).

Paul wasn't satisfied with his salvation or even with having a personal relationship with Jesus. He wanted more than that. He wanted to experience God's resurrection power in his life.

Paul's momma ain't raised no dummy. He knew that God had already blessed him with "every spiritual blessing in the heavenly places in Christ" (Ephesians 1:3). Now he just wanted to experience something that was already his. He was like an anxious kid at Christmas who already knows what mom and dad have wrapped up under the tree.

Please don't settle for mud pies because God is inviting you on an all-expense paid vacation in Hawaii. Forget what TLC said and go and chase those waterfalls. You shouldn't be taking life advice from R & B songs anyway.

2) Go on a LIFE Path Retreat

There's a lot of stuff here to work on. You need to set aside some time to focus on the assignments. It's best to do it all at once if possible.

For years, I have taken at least a half day to go off by myself to work of this. I usually do this at least twice a year. I recommend scheduling at least four straight uninterrupted hours to be alone to work through the steps.

I have created a *LIFE Path Guide* that you can download for free. You are free to use it and distribute to others as well. This guide will lead you through the steps to create your *LIFE Path*. You can download this guide from my website for free (**www.thiendoan.net/lifepathguide**).

The first thing you need to do is find a day on the calendar. Try to do it within the next two weeks so the information stays fresh. Download and print out the guide on actual paper and use it to complete your *LIFE Path*. When you're done, it will be around 7-10 pages long. Mine is nine pages. It's not something you can throw together randomly. It will take some focused effect. I've found that it is best to do it in one focused session.

3) Find Fellow Travelers

J.I. Packer opens his famous book *Knowing God* with a useful illustration. He said that on the path of life there are two types of people: people who are walking on the path and spectators who are watching from the balcony.

The people on the balcony have an elevated point of view. They shout opinions and instructions to the travelers down below. They think because they can see further down the path they know what it's like on the path. They don't. Don't listen to them. They're not making any progress on the path at all because they're not even on the path.

If you're a traveler on the path, ignore those folks

on the balcony. They cannot relate to what it's like on the path. Find yourself a community of fellow travelers on the path. We all need community for encouragement, direction, and even correction.

I've created a private group on Facebook for readers of this book to interact with one another. This is intended to be a safe place to ask questions and interact with me and other readers. If you get stuck writing your eulogy, or if you need some ideas, come to the group, and post your question. Perhaps you'll be able to find the answers you're looking for and a community to walk with.

To join this Facebook group, just go to the group page and click to join the group. It's free to join and I hope to connect with you on this group page.

You can join the Facebook group by going to this link: **www.facebook.com/groups/lifepathbook**.

4) Feed Your Brain

If you're not learning, you're not growing as a person. You need to continue to invest in yourself. I encourage you to start a reading habit if you don't have one. Start by getting good books and reading for ten minutes a day.

Below is a list of some of the resources I referred to in this book:

The One Thing by Gary Keller
Living Forward by Michael Hyatt
The Path Principle by Andy Stanley
Visioneering by Andy Stanley
Good to Great by Jim Collins
Four Disciplines of Execution by FranklinCovey
Seven Habits of Highly Effective People by Stephen Covey
How to Fail at Almost Everything by Scott Adams
The Miracle Morning by Hal Elrod
The Creative Habit by Twyla Tharp
The Power of Habit by Charles Duhigg
Mini Habits by Stephen Guise
Do Over by Jon Acuff
Lasting Impact by Carey Nieuwhof

It's so easy today to get good books. We live in the information age. I read at least three books a week, sometimes even ten or more. And I don't buy most of them. I primarily read books on my Amazon Kindle reading device that I get from my library through an app called Overdrive. It's amazing! I can check out books from the library from my phone or computer and the book magically appears on my Kindle. And it's free! You don't have to buy a Kindle either. If you have a tablet or smartphone, you can download the Kindle app for free also.

I also signed up for Amazon Kindle Unlimited which is like NetFlix for eBooks. Currently, it costs $10 a month and I can check out ten books at a time.

I also enjoy listening to audiobooks. I subscribe to Audible which is Amazon's audiobook division. Audible is expensive, but you can get your first book free if you click this link (www.audible.com). You can also download audiobooks you check out from the library on the Overdrive app.

Another way I feed my brain is to listen to podcasts. Podcasts are like indie radio shows on different topics. If all else fails, get your butt to the library and check out a book. You pay for that dang thing with your taxes. You might as well use it.

You have no excuse not to feed your brain. Momma always says, "Stupid is as stupid does."

5) Help others find their LIFE Path.

The best way to learn something is when you have to teach it someone else. That's how I feel when I have to help my kids with their homework.

There are people all around you who are drifting aimlessly through life. They are Christian zombies wandering mindlessly in life's cul-de-sac looking for something to satisfy their hunger. Help them. (By the way, here's a hilarious video about adopting a millennial at **https://youtu.be/RGvrmltfMrA**).

For years, I've been meeting with a bunch of guys for breakfast on Tuesday mornings. I led them through the *LIFE Path* process and kept them accountable. I encourage you to read this book with someone else. Take them through the exercises.

6) Review, Revise, Rinse and Repeat

This is an iterative process. That means it's something that you keep on doing and improving. I've been doing this for well over a decade straight. I constantly review my *LIFE Path*. I revise it and update it at least twice a year. And I repeat this process over and over, tweaking and improving it each time.

One of the things that have helped me most is that I read a portion of my *LIFE Path* first thing each morning. I have a copy on my desk at my office. Reading it reminds me of what is important, what is a priority and what is not. It also inspires me to put in some good work because I want to achieve that legacy that I wrote about. I encourage you to review yours daily too.

I also encourage you to schedule another *LIFE Path Retreat* six months from now. This is where you can evaluate your progress and adjust your goals if needed. Keep on repeating this process. Make it part of your yearly rhythm.

7) Join the "Inner Circle"

I want to thank you for allowing me to take you on this journey. The primary reason I wrote this book is that this process has been so helpful to me. I wanted to pass it on to you.

I hope that it has been helpful to you. I would love to connect with you and hear any stories you may have.

Go to my website. I have a bunch of FREE resources available. There's hours of videos of my teaching, workshops, PDF downloads, PowerPoint slides, and much more. But I don't want to give these resources away to just anyone. They are only available for my "Inner Circle."

The Inner Circle is password-protected portion of my website that will contain all my FREE resources. Here's the website address:

www.thiendoan.net/resources

Can I ask for a favor?

Thanks for reading my book. I do have a favor to ask. This is an independently published book and I don't have a marketing department or a budget for advertisement. The only way this book won't get lost in the digital ether is if you leave a review on Amazon (hopefully 5 stars).

It will only take you a minute and you can always go back and edit your review later. It would help me a lot if you even wrote, "Book Good" on a review. Just be honest. So, can you do me a solid and leave a review?

Thank you. I really appreciate it. I look forward to connecting with you in the future.

Many blessings,
Thien

WANT A FREE RESOURCES?

Go to my website:
thiendoan.net/resources

Code: Lakers

Made in the USA
Lexington, KY
19 September 2017